*Joyce Neville*

# How to Share Your Faith Without Being Offensive

**Revised Edition**

MOREHOUSE PUBLISHING
WILTON, CONNECTICUT

Dedicated to
**My Wonderful Husband, Edwin**
with Whom I Share Christ, Life, Love, Ministry

*Revised edition published in 1989 by*
Morehouse Publishing Company
78 Danbury Road
Wilton, Connecticut 06897

**Library of Congress Cataloging in Publication Data**
Neville, Joyce.
  How to share your faith without being offensive/Joyce Neville.
  p.   cm.
  Reprint. Originally published: New York: Seabury Press, 1979.
  ISBN 0-8192-1479-5
  1. Witness bearing (Christianity)   I. Title.
BV4520.N39   1989                                                    89-3291
248 '.5—dc20                                                              CIP

*Printed in the United States of America*
                        by
              BSC LITHO
           Harrisburg, PA

Scripture quotations in this book marked RSV are from the Revised Standard Version of the Bible, Copyright 1946, 1952, © 1971, 1973 by the Division of Christian Education of the National Council of the Churches of Christ in the U.S.A. Used by permission.

Verses marked TLB are taken from The Living Bible, copyright 1971 by Tyndale House Publishers, Wheaton, Ill. Used by permission.

The verse marked GNB is from the Good News Bible—New Testament: Copyright © American Bible Society 1966, 1971, 1976. Used by permission.

# Contents

## Part Two: CHRISTIAN SMALL GROUPS or How to Participate in a Small Group without Being Offended  69

*Part One*

# Christian Verbal Witness

## OR HOW TO SHARE YOUR FAITH WITHOUT BEING OFFENSIVE

# 1

# Three-pronged Witness:
# Telling, Doing, Being

EVERY Christian has a sacred story uniquely his own, even if he has not thought of it in those terms. This sacred story is comprised of many sacred chapters, some short, some long, some about happy experiences, some about sad ones. As Christians, our life story is a book written by God, a book to be shared as well as lived.

While words are not a substitute for action, neither is action a substitute for words, as the Reverend Claxton Monro says in his book, *Witnessing Laymen Make Living Churches:* "The total witness that one can give involves his life—the way he lives and dies—and his words—the things he says. . . . Sincere, faithful Christian obedience is a prerequisite for any spoken witness. But we need to be reminded, on the other hand, that no one can claim to live a life so good that he merits a right to speak for Christ. . . . Christians speak because they feel compelled of God, or called to do so, and hope that someone will be helped by what they have to say."[1]

But it has been my experience in many years of involvement in the ministry of verbal witness that members of mainstream churches—Catholic, Anglican, and Protestant —respond to the word *witness* in terms of offensive images.

Scenes come to mind of great emotionalism, open confession of sin, self-righteous aggressiveness, and negative personal challenges encased in theology that puts God in a box and people in spiritual strait jackets. Nothing could be further from the truth, and it is one of the purposes of this book to show that the verbal Christian witness, in its original, pure and true form, is none of these.

Witnessing, as evolved in the apostolic church and practiced in today's mainstream churches in worship services, small groups, and one to one, is intelligent, beautiful, uplifting, informative, freeing, and in good taste. This kind of witnessing began returning to the church in the 1920s under the leadership of the late Reverend Samuel M. Shoemaker, rector of Calvary Episcopal Church, New York City.* Since then, millions of Christians of all denominations have learned to witness to their faith in a quiet, natural, and extremely effective way.

Yet, after every course I taught on witnessing in the Lay Ministry Training Program for the Episcopal Diocese of Western New York, people in the class invariably said, "I didn't know it was like this!" and "I had no idea this was witnessing!" Many Christians who share their faith verbally are witnessing and do not even know it. Others do not share their faith verbally for fear of being offensive.

Nevertheless, mainstream Christians have sought to share their faith in other ways and there has been much said by our churches in the past couple of decades about "doing." They have felt that the "doing" was a witness to the "being." In a sense, all our social action, political action, volunteer service, and helpful things we do for others are a witness to our "being." But the evangelistic impact, if any, is so implicit that it is not explicit most of the time. Agnostics, atheists, humanists, people of other religions do the same things. So "doing" may

---

*Refer to the biography, *I Stand by the Door: The Life of Sam Shoemaker*, by Helen Smith Shoemaker (Waco, Tex.: Word Books, 1967); and *The Breeze of the Spirit: Sam Shoemaker and the Story of Faith at Work*, by Irving Harris (Hantsport, Nova Scotia, Lancelot Press, 1980).

or may not be a Christian witness in itself, although all Christians must express their Christianity in some "doing"—in whatever ministries to which God calls them—in order to give a complete witness for Christ.

However, "doing" is not the same as "telling." During the past few decades, as leaders and grass roots members in the mainstream churches increasingly have called for viable evangelism programs, those participating in established activities within these churches—from social action organizations to denominational publications—have been claiming that what they are doing is evangelism. The reasons for this are that they do not understand evangelism, they want to retain their status and influence, and they want more budget allocations. But these groups are not evangelizing. They are serving. They are "doing," not "telling." They are giving an action witness, not a verbal witness, most of the time.

"Everything the Church does is not evangelism," writes the Rev. A. Wayne Schwab, Evangelism and Renewal Officer for the Episcopal Church:

Evangelism is an identifiable, unique activity. It centers in the presentation of Jesus Christ (encounter with Him) and the response of faith (commitment to Him and responsible membership in His Church). Liturgy, education, social ministry may have evangelistic elements but they are not evangelism. . . . The Episcopal Church tends to mistake ministry to persons in need and work for social justice as evangelism. These must be done but they are not evangelism. We seem to have lost confidence in the message to stand on its own. While it must always be lovingly presented, the Gospel does go beyond whatever works of love and justice we do in its name.[2]

Although written in an Episcopal Church context, this statement applies to all Christian bodies and we are beginning to recognize the truth of it.

"Evangelism is the presentation of Jesus Christ, in the power of the Holy Spirit, in such ways that persons may be led to believe in Him as Savior and follow Him as Lord within the fellowship of His Church." This is the definition of evangelism adopted by the Episcopal Church's General Convention in 1973. It is a good definition, but still many people hold negative images about evangelism and witnessing. They do not want "revivals," they do not want to go door to door "soul winning," and they certainly are not going to stand out on the street, preaching—the only images of evangelism they have.

There are many methods of evangelism which are nothing like these, and verbal witnessing—the right kind—is one. Evangelism is not the only purpose of witnessing (see the next chapter), and "telling" is only part of our witness as Christians; but to give a total witness, the "telling" must come in somewhere, some way, at some time. If you "be" silently, people may love you and think you are wonderful. You may "do," but who will know why you give of yourself, your time, your money for some worthy purpose? They will think you are just a great person who cares about people. In that case, you are a witness for yourself.

Rosalind Rinker, author of *You Can Witness with Confidence,* writes: "Our testimony must be both in deed and in word. The spoken word is never really effective unless it is backed up by the life. The living deed is ultimately inadequate without the spoken word. The reason for this is obvious. No life is good enough to speak for itself. Any person who says, 'I don't need to witness; I just let my life speak,' is unbearably self-righteous."[3]

In order to have a Christian witness to tell, you must, of course, "be" a Christian in your thoughts, beliefs, and lifestyle, which are reflected by what you say and do. Christian thinking involves a sense of inner peace, an attitude of spiritual joy, and a response of compassionate love toward others. Christian beliefs involve centering your life in Christ, letting the Holy Spirit work through you, and growing in understanding of the triune God as expressed in the Bible and taught by the church. Christian lifestyle involves ministry to others, clean speaking, moral behavior, and refraining from participation in conversations and actions of a low spiritual consciousness.

None of us is going to live up to an absolute standard in all ways, of course. We often are prone to speak and act in ways that our non-Christian associates expect, or to respond to daily problems without thinking about God's will and asking His guidance. I like a definition of sin I heard which says that sin is doing what you want to do when you know God wants you to do something else. Who has not fallen into that situation? We cannot expect to be sinless, but if we know we are redeemed, in that knowledge we can live a Christian life. I call myself a "working-at-it" Christian, the kind that is described on some buttons seen at renewal weekends that say, "PBPGIFWMY"— Please Be Patient, God Isn't Finished With Me Yet!

While in a way a silent Christian life is a witness to Christ, yet, as Sam Shoemaker wrote in *Creating Christian Cells:* "I cannot, by being good, tell of Jesus' atoning death and resurrection nor of my faith in His divinity. The emphasis is too much on me and too little on Him."[4]

If, in our "being" and in our "doing," we accept opportunities that open to us to share verbally what Christ means to us and what He has done in our life—"telling"—then we are giving a total witness for Christ. I believe Christ wants our total witness.

Listening to the witnesses of those who took my classes has reinforced my conviction that the church isn't dead—it's alive, but it just doesn't talk about it. A survey taken in one parish revealed that clergy and laity alike were surprised that their spiritual stories would be of interest to anyone, especially to the church at large. But as the Reverend Douglas C. Blackwell points out in *Relay* (the Aurora Conference Centre's resource periodical), the Bible is "really a vast and timeless collection" of personal stories, illustrating that our stories relate to God's story in our everyday experience. "Because of Him, my journey and your journey not only make sense—they are redeemed and made brilliantly new with possibility. . . . Together, His story will give new life to us both and will enrich that larger story which belongs to all the people of God."[5]

# 2

# The Three Purposes of Verbal Witness

VERBAL witness serves three purposes:

It is an evangelism ministry to unbelievers.
It is a strengthening ministry to Christians.
It is a unifying ministry in an ecumenical age.

Those of us who have been deeply involved in the witnessing ministry have seen over and over its fantastic effectiveness, especially when practiced within the witnessing community of the church. It is effective with unbelievers, nominal church-goers, and committed Christians alike, although its predominant dynamic is as an evangelism ministry.

People who cannot be reached through the Bible, or the sacraments, or good preaching and teaching, people who may reject these elements, cannot deny that the person sharing an experience of God's action in his life has had that experience. Here is evidence, shown in a person's life as well as in his words. The skeptic can say, "That won't work for me," but he cannot say, "That didn't happen to you." Frequently, he says, "If that happened to you, maybe it could happen to me."

I can name countless people who had their first encounter with Christ through listening to a layperson witness, usually in a small meeting in a home or church, or even in an office or jail! Often it happened on a one-to-one basis.

Witnessing is also a ministry used, on a continuing basis, by Christians with other Christians. In this context, it is often not thought of as a ministry, even though it serves that function. It is done simply for the joy of one person sharing with another what God has been doing in his life. In this context, a witness is like a gift given out of love—the giving brings joy to both the giver and receiver. In the sharing and in the hearing, both are being raised to a higher consciousness; both are reminded of the centrality of the gospel in life; both are re-affirmed in the knowledge of a today God who acts in our personal experience; both are strengthened in faith, love, joy, trust and other fruits of the Spirit.

When done as a ministry to another Christian who is troubled, bereaved or sick, the effects of a witness go even deeper, especially when the witness becomes a key that unlocks the door to problem solving and healing, which I have very often seen happen. It happens because the witness brings new spiritual insight in some way to the sufferer.

When used in small group situations, the witness gets its point across in a graphic way, which is easy to comprehend and to remember.

Those of us who are interested in the ecumenical movement wonder if the many denominations are going to have unity or uniformity, or either! I personally think we already have much unity and will have more. I don't think we will ever have uniformity, and, as far as I am concerned, this is a good thing.

We have unity in a number of ways with which we are familiar—joint services on special days, working together in inter-church organizations and social action projects, etc. This is outward unity. One way in which we are united inwardly is through verbal witness. When people of different denominations share what Christ is doing in their lives and what He means to them in a personal way—not Biblical, doctrinal, or theological concepts—then all denominational barriers fall away and all are on one level of communication.

An interesting experience of this kind happened to me when I was working in an institution owned and operated by a doctrinally strict denomination. I (an Episcopalian) often had lunch with groups of these Christians and discovered that they took a rather dim view of the eternal future of Episcopalians and Roman Catholics. Instead of arguing with them, I simply shared what Jesus Christ was doing in my life—He answered prayers, He gave me guidance, He gave me creative inspiration in my publications work—and other ways in which I felt God was helping me. Their response would be, "My goodness, you sound just like one of us!"

On the other end of the spectrum, I was once a member of a Bible study group in which everyone else, except my husband and myself, was Roman Catholic. We used different versions of the Bible as we studied together, and we never discussed issues of obvious doctrinal differences. What we did do was to help one another acquire a better understanding of what happened in the gospels, epistles, and even in the book of Revelation. We shared how those events and teachings were affecting our lives today and how those truths, applied to our lives, were making a difference. We also prayed for one another and shared our concerns and answers.

This is not to say that we should not have ecumenical groups discussing Bible, theology, and doctrine. These groups are very meaningful and unifying to the extent that we attain a better understanding of other denominational concepts. We need such dialogue to be well educated Christians. However, it is not unifying in the same way as the sharing of Christian experience.

Witnessing, then, adds a dimension and a depth to many different life situations, which could not be experienced in any other way. Increasingly, Christians are beginning to realize that they need the ability to share their personal faith with others. As Bishop William H. Folwell, of the Episcopal Diocese of Central Florida, said, "It is time we learned once again what it means to tell somebody else what Jesus Christ means to us as Lord and Savior in our lives. It is time for us to learn to expect that the Holy Spirit will teach us what to say when we don't know what to say so that we speak openly and boldly with great confidence about the glorious majesty of God, the great love of God revealed in Christ Jesus, and this holy fellowship brought about by the outpouring of the Holy Spirit."[1]

# 3

# What a Witness Is (and Isn't)

WHAT exactly is this verbal witness we are talking about?

Webster's Dictionary defines the word *witness* as that which serves as evidence, or furnishes evidence or proof; one who beholds, or otherwise has personal knowledge of, anything; to bear testimony; to give evidence; to observe with one's own eyes or ears.[1] (In its definition, Webster's uses *witness* both for what is told and for the person who tells it. In my definition of a Christian witness, I use *witness* for what is told and *witnesser* for the teller, for clarity.)

A Christian witness is a story of God's action in one's personal life or a description of what being a Christian means in a personal way. When a person shares verbally with another person something about his ongoing interaction with God in Christ, relating some way in which God's power has been manifested in his life or God's nature has been revealed to him, he is giving a Christian witness. A witnesser shares experiences and insights resulting from either his conversion to Christ or his lifelong walk with Christ, and growing out of his living personal relationship with the Father, Son, and Holy Spirit. A witness may be told in a few words or many. It may include background information relevant to the circumstances of the experience.

A witnesser is not preaching, teaching, or exhorting. He is not interpreting scripture, theology, or doctrine. He is not telling the story of Jesus' life *on earth,* but of Jesus' life *in him.* A witness is not a recital from a book or a story about what God did for someone else or what the witnesser did for God. It is not a statement of opinion or a judgment of others. A witness is not a confession of sins, or the relating of embarrassing personal information, but it is always in good taste. A *good* Christian witness is always told in honesty, humility, and love. It may have sad or humorous aspects, but is never overemotional or offensive in any way, and is never forced on anyone for any reason. It leaves the listener free to accept it or reject it as applicable to his own life. A *good* witness is a joy to the Lord!

There are two ways you can witness. One is the biographical witness in which you relate the story of your spiritual life. The other is the single-story witness in which you relate one experience you have had in which God had a definite part or did a particular thing. The biographical witness will be the narrative either of how you came into your faith in the first place, how this experience changed your life, and the results since, or of how you have grown in the faith all your life and what your spiritual milestones have been. Usually, the opportunities God gives you to share your faith with another will call for the single-story type of witness—a particular experience in your life that meets a particular need in another's life or is on a subject of interest to another.

# 4

# What to Witness about—39 Subjects

THESE are subjects for verbal witness. Although most witnesses will fall under one or more of these topics, subjects for witness are as endless as the ways God acts in our lives. Do not try to confine your witnesses to these subjects, but use them as a guide to catalyze your awareness of the many-faceted ways our Lord is active in your life.

1. If there ever was a time when you made a conscious commitment of your life to Christ, how did this come about? What did it mean to you at the time? Has it made a difference in your life since? In what ways?

2. If you have always been a committed Christian, what are some experiences which you feel were steps forward in your growth in faith, knowledge, and love of God?

3. If you believe that God has a plan for your life, how do you see it working out in your experience? In what ways have you discovered God's plan as you have gone along?

4. In what ways do you feel that God is helping you to grow in emotional and spiritual maturity?

5. At what times in your life has Christ been most real to you?

6. Have you ever experienced a strong awareness of God's presence? How did it happen? What did it mean to you and how did it help you?

7. What was the most vivid experience of prayer you ever had? At what times in your life was prayer most meaningful to you?

8. What personal experiences have you had which you feel indicate that you have a personal relationship with Jesus Christ?

9. What are some ways in which God has strengthened your faith? What were the personal experiences through which He did this?

10. Has another Christian ever shared his personal faith experiences with you in such a way that it gave you new insight or helped with a problem or made a difference in some way to you? How did it help you?

11. Have you ever shared your personal faith experiences with the same results? How did it help the other person?

12. How has God given you peace in a difficult situation or unhappy time?

13. How has Christ enabled you to make Him the center of your life?

14. If you feel that Christ is the head of your household, as St. Paul taught, how does this work out in daily living with your family? What effect does it have on your marriage relationship? On your relationship with your children? On your relationship with a friend or family member with whom you live?

15. In what ways do you feel God helps you in your business relationships? In your social relationships?

16. How has God enabled you to love a person who does things of which you don't approve?

17. What was an experience in which you grew in wisdom, understanding, and trust of God?

18. Have you had an experience in which Christ's love has changed your attitude or outlook? How did this come about?

19. Have you had experiences that show you how God enters

different aspects of your life, your plans, your actions? What were they?

20. Have you ever sought and received God's guidance? Did you follow your guidance? What happened?

21. Have you ever had to overcome resistance to what you felt was God's will on some matter in your life? Have you ever wanted one thing and felt God wanted another for you? How did you resolve it? What happened?

22. How has a verse of scripture influenced your life or helped you to understand God's will in a specific situation? Are you able to relate your Bible study to your personal life? How?

23. In Galatians 5:22, St. Paul says that the fruits of the Spirit are love, joy, peace, patience, kindness, goodness, faithfulness, gentleness, and self-control. In what ways have you experienced one or more of these fruits of the Spirit?

24. Have you had an experience in which prayer was the vehicle for changing resentment to forgiveness, or restoring a broken relationship, or learning to love someone you disliked? In what way did it work out?

25. Have you had an experience in which prayer was the vehicle for healing a negative state of mind, hatred, jealousy, envy, anxiety, anger, contempt, nervousness, confusion, frustration, etc.? How did this come about?

26. Have you had an experience in which Christ has brought you from fear to trust? guilt to forgiveness? insecurity to security? bondage to freedom? hurt to healing? rejection to acceptance? futility to creativity? alienation to reconciliation? a sense of unworthiness to appreciation of self-worth? a sense of aloneness to a sense of belonging in Christian community? How did this happen?

27. What are some specific examples of ways you have experienced the power of prayer? (i.e., you received what you prayed for; you received something better than you prayed for; you did not receive what you prayed for and you are thankful; you were relieved of an unhappy situation; you were not re-

lieved of an unhappy situation, but God gave you the fortitude, strength, peace, wisdom, patience, etc. to go through it; God protected you from a tragedy, illness, setback or mistake; God did not protect you from a tragedy, illness, setback or mistake, but He redeemed it in some way.)

28. Have you ever received a healing of illness—mental, emotional, or physical—through prayer alone? How did it come about?

29. What are some ways in which God has helped you in illness healed by conventional methods?

30. Have you experienced through prayer healing of a sin or fault or habit that is not too personal to share? How?

31. If you felt grief in the suffering and/or death of a loved one, in what ways do you feel Christ helped you through this experience? Do you feel your faith made a difference in your response to the tragedy? How?

32. What does the sacrament of Holy Communion mean to you in a personal way? Did you ever receive a special grace through the Eucharist? What effect did this have on your faith or in your life?

33. How has Holy Unction, Sacramental Confession, Baptism, or any other sacrament helped you in a specific way at a certain time?

34. If you belong to a small group that meets regularly for worship, study, witnessing, or prayer, what does it mean to you and how does it help you?

35. Do you practice regular private prayer, meditation, and spiritual reading? In what ways has this helped you in your spiritual growth?

36. Do you pray regularly for others? Is this a meaningful experience? In what ways?

37. Do you feel that the Lord has called you to a lay ministry? How did He do this? How has He helped you in its performance? How has He helped you in other ways in ministering to others?

38. Do you tithe part of your income to God's work in the church and the world? Have you found this to be a meaningful experience? Do you feel that your tithing is related to the meeting of your own material needs? How?

39. In what specific ways do you feel the Holy Spirit helps you to speak and act so that your daily life is a Christian witness?

# 5

# How to Witness—21 Guidelines

ALTHOUGH any Christian can witness without training since he is relating personal experience, effective verbal witnessing is a skill to be cultivated by most of us. Some people are more gifted at this than others, but all of us can improve our effectiveness by using common-sense guidelines. I have developed these guidelines from thousands of good—and bad—witnesses I have heard over the years since I became involved in this ministry in 1954.

1. Be specific, not vague. Do not speak in generalities.

2. Show clearly what part God, prayer or faith took in the experience.

3. Speak in terms the listener understands—in his own language. Avoid religious clichés and jargon.

4. Be honest. Do not embellish the story, exaggerate or over-dramatize. Mention failures, doubts, inadequacies. Imply that you, as a Christian, do not feel superior, but have the same problems as anyone else, while sharing how God gives you victory over them and how He is making you a better person than you could be on your own.

5. Tell your experience in such a way that it has substance and does not come across as being primarily an emotional expe-

rience. Emotions may be expressed as appropriate, however, as emotions are part of all experience.

6. Speak matter-of-factly as if you were relating any other kind of experience. There is no need to feel timid or be aggressive just because you are speaking of spiritual things. Bring in humor where appropriate. Be relaxed.

7. Speak only to the particular point under discussion with experiences along that line. Give your biographical witness only when appropriate or if questions lead to it. Share only what the listener needs to hear. Don't answer questions he doesn't ask.

8. Say just enough to give the picture without going into great detail or sidetracking onto tangents.

9. The major part of your witness should always be on "what happened" rather than on "how bad it was." Do not relate experiences of sin, sorrow, sickness, depression, and the like in such a way that your witness becomes a tale of woe. Simply state what the problem was, its acuteness, its longevity, and how God resolved it or helped you through it.

10. Leave the listener free to accept or reject your witness as valid for him. As Rosalind Rinker says, "Everyone is as stubborn about having religion thrust down his throat as you are! The human heart wants to make its own discoveries. But sometimes it wants someone who is an expert in gentleness to help. . . . We need freedom to believe! Freedom to live! We also need freedom to listen, to ask questions, to share, and to search." [1]

11. Since witnessing is not preaching, teaching, or exhorting, don't tell others what they should do, believe, or say. If you hear yourself saying "you should" or "you must" or other such phrases, you are off the track and will usually meet with resistance unless they are seeking your spiritual guidance.

12. Admit you don't have all the answers about God or all the answers to life. Christ *is* the Answer and *has* the answers, but we don't have all the answers about the Answer! Your listener will respect you and what you say if you avoid giving

"pat" answers and if you are not judgmental or self-righteous.

13. Never tell anyone that they should have spiritual experiences similar to yours. Each person must grow in his own way on his own spiritual path. Only God knows what his path is. He may be on *his* path even though it seems to you that he is going in the wrong direction. God can use you to open spiritual doors and plant spiritual seeds, and that is your purpose in witnessing.

14. Do not criticize other people, churches, religions, or systems of thought. Barriers are built by criticism. Instead of saying why you think others are wrong or misled, acknowledge whatever spiritual truths you can in the other belief that has been expressed and emphasize what difference your own Christian faith has made in your life. The positive approach is always more loving and convincing than the negative. You can show an interest in their views without compromising your own.

15. Do not relate mystical experiences unless (1) you do it in a clearly understandable way, and (2) it had a profound effect for good in your life and you tell about the results. Witness to people on subjects that are on *their* spiritual level, not *yours*. The majority cannot relate to "far-out" religious experience and will turn off this approach.

16. Incompleted experiences should not be shared as witnesses. (e.g., ". . . and so I'm praying about this and doing what God guides me to do and I know God is going to work it out in such-and-such a way.") Wait until God does work it out to share the experience. Otherwise, it usually will not be very meaningful to the listener, and it may not work out in the way you expect it to.

17. A witness is not a story of what we are doing for God, but what God is doing for us. In witnessing about lay ministry, we should stress God's help in guiding us to it and in its performance, and give God the major credit for any good results, which is where the credit really belongs, anyway.

18. Do not relate another's personal witness except in instances where another's experience exactly fits the need ex-

pressed. Even then, never tell something about another person that is very personal, that would embarrass or hurt him. Personal things people share with you should always be kept confidential. It is usually best not to tell another's witness unless you have heard him give it in public.

19. A witness is not a confession of sins, so do not tell experiences of a deeply personal nature, such as specific sexual experiences, that would embarrass you or the listener. If you are open to the Holy Spirit's guidance, you will know whether you are to share something of a very personal nature with another person. If he has shared a problem with you, similar to one over which God has given you a victory or helped you in some major way, you may feel that by entering fully into his search for an answer you can help him. In such a case you may feel right about sharing something too personal to be shared otherwise. The keys here are guidance and common sense.

20. By the same token that you do not make a confession of sins when you witness, never be judgmental about another's sins that he may confess to you, which sometimes happens in a spiritual sharing context. He will feel guilty and repentant as the Holy Spirit leads him, and that is not your responsibility. But he will need confirmation of your love and your acceptance of him as a person and possibly your guidance as to what he should do to seek a healing. On the other hand, never pretend you approve of sinful or unloving behavior—this negates what you could do to help. Sometimes he will want you to pray with him asking God's forgiveness or guidance for him. You may direct him to a minister or counselor. You could give him a book you think would help him. In any case, let him see that God loves him and is present to help him.

21. Avoid a lot of quoting from the Bible or other books. Many people think they must quote a lot of Scripture to witness. To the contrary, it is better not to quote Scripture in a witness, especially when you are speaking informally to one or two people, unless you can show how it has applied directly to your

own life, and then only quote one or two verses. Too much Scripture quoting makes a witness impersonal and "teachy" or "preachy," and then you have defeated the very purpose of your witness, which is to relate what effect Christ has on your personal life. Quoting from a book, even the Bible, does not tell this. Your listener may know the Scriptures well, but he can find out only from your witness how it applies to your life. Although every Christian should acquire as much education in Scripture and theology as possible for his own understanding and for the ability to express concepts, some of the most moving witnesses are given by people new in the faith with little Christian education. They are able to share Christian experience because a witness is just that—experience, not concepts. (Expression of concepts, even informally, is teaching.) One can even minister to others, talk over their problems, and pray with them without education or training. But to grow in Christ, to cultivate skill in lay ministry, and to counsel in depth, Christian education in various forms is essential.

One of the best statements ever made about witnessing guidelines was that of Lee Whiston, a Congregational minister, author, and columnist for the nondenominational Christian magazine, *Faith/At/Work*. He said:

Tell your witness in story form, with all the characteristics of drama: contrast, suspense, vividness, punchline and climax. The story carries its own witness and power—there is no need to preach, or to drive it home, or to exhort! It tells what God has done. It gives credit and glory to God. It's personal. It's fresh in time and spirit. It speaks to the listener's need, not to his sins. It does not destroy faith, it builds faith. It's in intelligible and pungent English. It's alive and enthusiastic. It's always in good taste. It's brief. It includes encounter with God and with man.

What follows is the author's biographical witness, not meant to serve as a model, but as an example. Everyone's witness is uniquely his own. It was originally a letter, written in the summer of 1975, to the late Reverend Canon William O. Hanner, Episcopal priest, then retired in St. Petersburg, Florida. It was published in the December 1975 *New Life* magazine.[2]

Dear Father Hanner:

It was one of the highlights of my life to receive Christ's Body and Blood from your hands again at the altar rail last Sunday. The tears came because I was remembering all that has happened in my life in the twenty-two years since I last knelt before the altar to receive communion from you. My life has changed so much since then that it's as if I were living on a different planet. And you, dear Father, were my launching pad!

I am glad you remember me, but I'm not surprised you don't remember exactly what you did for me, knowing that you have done it for many before and after me. It is a joy to respond to your request for the story.

By way of background, I was brought up as an only child in a home where religion was not part of family life. I went to church and Sunday school now and then with friends of various denominations, and regularly for one year when I was eight years old and living with a Christian aunt and uncle. While attending college, I felt an urge to be baptized and join a church. I did not know why at the time, but years later my Christian grandmother mentioned that she always prayed for me. Knowing what I do now about prayer, I believe it was her prayers that drew me in that direction.

I went church-searching and one Sunday attended an Episcopal church. When the service was finished, I knew the Episcopal Church was where I belonged. I felt I had come home. I loved the beautiful liturgy, the majestic music, the kneeling for prayers—everything. So I attended confirmation class and was baptized and confirmed. The class was extremely dull—church history and a lot of dry material—but I forced myself to go through with it. Looking back, I know the Lord was responsible for my faithful attendance.

To me, being baptized and confirmed was an intellectual exercise. Becoming a Christian was an intellectual exercise. I decided, quite objectively, that I could accept the witness of the disciples and apostles, and therefore could accept Jesus as the Son of God. After my baptism and confirmation, I sighed with relief and told myself, "Now I'll go to heaven when I die!" I viewed baptism as a vaccination against hell. Christ was my Savior but not my Lord. I went to church only once a month for 11 o'clock Holy Communion because it made me feel good although the sermons were dull.

My life went on unchanged. It had always been unhappy and chaotic, completely ruled by extremes of emotions dictated by what others did and said concerning me. Things went from bad to worse in the next seven years and I was really messed up in so many ways. By then I had graduated from college, had my own apartment and was working. A friend in my office told me about the wonderful priest at St. Stephen's Church and what great sermons he gave.

On Christmas morning in 1952 I went to St. Stephen's because I was in such need and had to be in church even though I had attended the midnight service in my own parish. Your sermon made Christ come alive. I attended St. Stephen's every Sunday from then on and transferred my letter. However, even though Christ lived for me an hour a week and I clung desperately to the hope of His love and power, this still didn't make any change in my life. I didn't know how to apply it, and/or perhaps didn't want to, I don't know. I was too busy trying to make God do my will!

The following August I decided I would commit suicide. I wasn't trying to be dramatic or get even with anyone. I just wanted out. I began putting all my affairs in order and very calmly planning the method.

The Tuesday night before the weekend I was going to do this, you suddenly appeared at my door. I stared at you in surprise and, without even saying hello, exclaimed, "Father, what are you doing here?'' You replied, ''I just felt I should come to see you.'' (It was eighteen years later while talking with a childhood friend that I discovered she had called you, asking you to try to keep me from committing suicide, and you had kept her confidence. Since she claims to be a Jewish atheist, I asked her why she called *you,* and she replied, ''Well, you wouldn't listen to me, I thought you might listen to your priest!'')

You came in and we talked. I told you I was going to commit suicide because life was not worth living. I asked you if I would go to hell. This was an academic question because your answer wasn't going to make any difference. You said that was for God to decide, and then you told me the thing that saved my soul, saved my life and changed my life.

You said, ''Joyce, God has a plan for your life, and if you will surrender your life to Christ and ask Him for His blueprint for your life instead of giving Him your blueprint, you will find peace, joy, fulfillment, and happiness. You will find that life is worth living.'' I had never heard anything like this before, and I replied, ''But that's for ministers and missionaries, that's not for me.''

Then we talked for an hour. I don't remember what was said except that I insisted I knew what would make me happy and would make life worth living, and that your idea wouldn't work for me. I remember that I was so adamant that you finally had to give up talking to me, and you said that if I decided to take your suggestion, I should contact you.

After you left, I thought it over a lot. I remember that I turned on the radio and it was playing, ''You'll Never Walk Alone,'' and I thought that maybe God was trying to tell me something. I finally decided that I had nothing to lose and, if your idea didn't work, I could still commit suicide. (What a loving God we have, to honor a commitment to Him even with that attitude!)

So I called you and made an appointment to see you right

away. You said for me to make this commitment in the form of sacramental confession. I didn't know how that could work since I felt every problem in my life and all my unhappiness were caused by others. Nothing was ever my fault: I was perfect, I thought. So I went home and, for the first time in my life, I asked God to show me what I had done wrong against Him and other people. You had said to write it down. Well, I filled several pages in a steno notebook!

That weekend I came to confession. You sat on the inside of the altar rail and I knelt at the rail. I read aloud the confession form and all the things I had written down. However, I felt no real sense of guilt. It was strange. I knew I had done these things and I had to read the part that says I did them "by my own fault, by my own grievous fault," but I did not feel guilty—probably I was still subconsciously blaming everyone else.

Then, when you pronounced the absolution, I suddenly realized what a sinner I had been, I suddenly felt a tremendous sense of guilt as I saw my life from Christ's point of view, and I began to see myself for the first time. But in the same instant it was all lifted from me—suddenly. It was a great mystical experience. It happened in an instant. Verses of scripture that I had never understood flashed into my mind—"You must be born again" and "You shall know the truth and the truth shall make you free"—and I began to understand their meaning. In the years since, the depth of my understanding of these and other scriptures has increased many times over.

Then you said that for penance I should say this prayer: "Jesus, I love you, help me to love you more; Jesus, I trust you, help me to trust you more." During the following years, I can't tell you how many times I prayed that prayer, adding, "Jesus, I serve you, help me to serve you better," as He has given me ministries.

Then you left the church and I stayed there alone a long time, praying. I said, "God, my life isn't worth anything to me. If it's worth anything to you, take it, it's yours, do whatever you want to with it." He knew I meant it.

While there, I asked the Lord—for the first time in my life—what *He* wanted *me* to do. It came to me strongly that I should move to Houston, Texas, with two girl friends who had asked me to go with them but whom I had refused. I didn't know if this new spiritual life I had entered was real or if it would work, and I didn't know if I could survive without your help, but I knew even at that early stage that, if this were real, then it should not, and could not, depend on the help of any person on a continuing basis. It had to be able finally to stand on its own.

In October I moved to Houston where God gave me a whole new life that I never dreamed existed. After trying several Episcopal churches, I found St. Stephen's (the name was a divine coincidence) where the Reverend Claxton Monro was, and still is, rector. (He has since become, in my opinion, the Christian church's outstanding leader in evangelism, renewal, and lay ministry.) He also preached excellent sermons with real substance and was just beginning the prayer groups, witnessing, practice of specific Christian disciplines, exercise of lay ministries, and other related activities which have made this church such a powerhouse for Christ.

Without telling my whole story to him, I simply said that I had just given my life to Christ and asked, "Where do I go from here?" He put me into a weekly faith study and prayer fellowship group with six or eight other women, in which we discussed the Bible and many contemporary books on prayer, faith, Christian living, and spiritual healing. We talked about what God was doing in our daily lives and we prayed together spontaneously. Just from listening to them, I learned how to pray and got new insights into Scripture. I learned what God expected of me and what I could expect of Him.

For several months after arriving in Houston, I wasn't sure

this new spiritual way of life would work. One day I thought it would and the next day I thought it wouldn't. I received encouraging letters from you. I kept appearing at the church every time the doors opened—for worship, for study, for service projects, for social events.

Finally, with everything together, it jelled, and one morning I awakened feeling great joy and great peace and great freedom. I was possessed by the realization that it was all true—everything you had told me was true! I accepted it not only intellectually and emotionally but spiritually; not only consciously but subconsciously. It was just there, never to leave. I felt that my life was full of the Holy Spirit. Oh, yes, I've had my ups and downs like everyone, but that morning I knew I was "over the hump." God had sent me to another church in which all I heard and experienced reinforced all you had told me.

To tell you everything that has taken place since then would take many books. After eleven years in Houston, I moved to New York City to work for the Executive Council, at the Episcopal Church Center, for three years, and then I married Ed and moved to Buffalo where we now live. I have had some tough experiences and many exciting experiences. Other people, both clergy and laity, have meant more to me than I can tell, especially the late Right Reverend Michael Coleman, former Anglican Bishop of Qu'Appelle in Canada, who conducted many week-long missions in Houston and had a profound personal ministry to me, and Norman and Tot Atkinson of St. Stephen's, Houston, who counseled me wisely and taught me abundantly. I am also thankful for the people I have been able to help by God's grace. I am very thankful for the wonderful Christian husband God gave me, for to know him is to love him.

The other day, while I was thinking of my experience with you twenty-two years ago and my life since, I realized that when we give our lives to Christ, He does three things for us. He fulfills our needs, He gives us spiritual growth, and He gives us ministries. He does not accomplish these things in any particular order; rather all three areas overlap and are ongoing throughout our lives. (How's that for a sermon topic!)

One of Ed's favorite expressions is "Everything comes full circle." I felt it surely did last Sunday at the Eucharist with you. I felt that I was resealed in Christ, this time with my husband. When I think what you did for me and realize that, in one way or another, you have done it for many others through the years of your priesthood, I rejoice!

Thank you for last Sunday with you and your lovely wife, Rose. We loved being with you both. We pray for many more happy, fruitful years ahead for you.

Agape,
Joyce

# 6

# What Qualifies Us to Witness

ONE cannot convert others to that to which he himself is unconverted,"[1] wrote The Very Reverend Robert B. Hall, former Dean of St. Paul's Cathedral, Oklahoma City, in his manual, *Sharing Your Faith*. "In order to witness to the power of God, you must experience that power; in order to witness to the joy of a close, loving relationship with the Son of God, you must have such a relationship."[2]

The most essential condition for being a witness for Christ is that we must be totally committed to Him. He must be the Lord of our life as well as the Savior of our soul. It is impossible to have a meaningful relationship with our Lord if our faith is by intellectual assent only, as necessary as that is. Consciously living with Him, studying about Him, communicating with Him in prayer, seeking and following His guidance daily—this is our loving response to the One who wants our total self.

Having this commitment, we must be able to communicate it to others as it concerns our daily life. We must be able to share verbally *specific* ways in which we have experienced God's love, presence, power, guidance, strengthening, joy, and peace.

We need to know in a deep and abiding way that Christ *is* the answer and *has* the answers. He is the answer to life's meaning, and He guides us and helps us in finding answers to temporal problems. These answers may include the "doing" part of being a witness.

Not only must we believe that Christ is the answer and has the answers, but we must be willing to say so. As Christians, it is our calling and responsibility to say so when the opportunity arises. The best way to recognize and use these opportunities is to pray that we will be open to them. This is a prayer that is always answered. As Dean Hall said, "When you are ready to witness, when you are willing to witness, and when you have something to witness about, God will provide you with someone to whom to witness."[3]

Once I took a taxi in New York City, and when I told the driver that my destination was the Church of the Resurrection, he commented, "It would be nice to believe that, wouldn't it?" Sliding right into that opportunity, I said, "Well, I do believe it because it happened to me—not a physical resurrection, but a resurrection of my life." Then I went on to tell him how Christ had completely changed my life when I totally surrendered it to Him several years before. I never knew if the seed I planted contributed to a spiritual harvest later, but that is God's business, not mine.

Whenever I witness, I pray silently that the Holy Spirit will guide me. It is essential that what we say be what God knows the other person needs to hear, in the way he needs to hear it. If we pray for this, it will happen. "Don't try to witness *for* God; let Him do it *through* you,"[4] wrote Dean Hall. "Two things will surprise you about your witness. One is the way you will come up with expressions and illustrations that you've never thought of before. . . . The other thing is that you will be surprised at what God can do with your witness when you think it has been quite imperfect."[5]

The most striking instance I have had like this was at a time several years after my life-changing experience, when I was going through a crisis. Although I knew Christ had done some amazing things in my life and in the lives of countless friends, I felt very far away from Him because it seemed as if He had turned away from me. Although I knew intellectually that God does not operate this way, my emotions made me feel as if He did. At that time, I frequently had lunch with an employee at the institution in which I worked, since we often happened to be in the cafeteria at the same time. He shared with me many personal and family problems that were making him miserable, which were compounded by his illness, chronic leukemia. I was faced by a dilemma: I knew God wanted me to help him and I wanted to with all my heart, but feeling as I did, how could I?

What I did was simply to share all that God had done in my life and all I had learned about Him up to my crisis. I realized that no matter how I felt then, nothing could change what God had already done and what I had learned through that. A few months before he died, he moved to another city. Before he left, he came by my office and told me, "I just want to thank you for all you've done for me. What you said changed my life." I was astounded. Seldom before or since has God's power been shown to me so clearly. God had spoken to his needs through words that I knew in my mind were true but did not feel in my heart at the time I spoke them. I realized that if God could use me like that at such a time, how much more He could accomplish through me under normal circumstances. This experience helped me emerge from my crisis. Witnessing works both ways!

The Holy Spirit opens the other person to Christ's touch if He guides us to speak in His name. Whether or not we seem to get a response, we have obeyed God and planted a spiritual seed. Obedience is our responsibility; results are God's responsibility. Dean Hall said, "When you get ready to . . . tell others about God's activities in your life, the Holy Spirit not only goes with you, He goes before you. When you are led to speak of these things to a person, you will not be, as a salesman would call it, working 'cold turkey.' The Holy Spirit will already have been at work in the heart and mind of the one to whom you are led to speak, the soil will have been prepared in some measure for the seed which you are ready to plant."[6]

This came true in my experience several years ago when my grandfather, who was living in a distant state, was nearing death. The family had told me that he would never "talk religion" with them, although they had all tried at one time or another. Now he was so deaf that he could hear only if shouted at. Nevertheless, I felt God's urging to go visit him. As I sat down on his bed and held his hand, I prayed silently that if God wanted me to say something spiritual, He would provide an opening. The first words my grandfather spoke were, "Joyce, you know I'm not going to be here much longer." I knew this was the opening I had prayed for. Shouting, I shared briefly with him what Christ meant to me and assured him that Jesus loved him and would be with him in the next life as He was in this. His response was that he believed this. Several months later, my aunt told me that when he died, he told my grandmother, "I'll be waiting for you."

We should not worry about making a mistake when we witness. If we say the wrong thing, or the right thing comes out in the wrong way, or our timing is wrong, we should be aware that God redeems the mistakes we make while trying to follow His guidance in a loving and gentle way. Abiding by the preceding twenty-one guidelines in Chapter 5 will prevent most mistakes, and you will find they become second nature as you gain witnessing experience. God also expects us to use the common sense He gave us. St. Paul talks of being "fools for Christ," but he did not say anything about being "foolish" for Christ. There is a difference!

# 7

# Barriers to Witnessing

A dozen barriers prevent Christians from talking about their faith, but all can be overcome by a better understanding of witnessing and its purposes.

Our lack of awareness of unexpected opportunities is a common barrier. That chance remark, that relating of a frustration or problem, that sudden turn of the conversation when another opens himself more fully to us—these are unexpected opportunities God gives us to share His love with another. If we let such an opening go by, the moment may not come again to help that person spiritually. Our awareness will be developed as the desire grows within us to help others come into a closer relationship to God and as the realization breaks upon us that we can do it.

I have a good friend, an interior decorator and a beautiful Catholic Christian, whose faith has brought her through great tragedy and big problems. One day she mentioned that she was amazed how many clients kept her hours overtime telling her their heartaches. Some even called her to come back after her job was finished so that they would have someone with whom to share their burdens. So I said, "What a wonderful opportunity for you to witness to them about what your faith has meant to you!" Surprised, she replied, "Oh, I never thought of that!"

Even if we are aware that an opportunity has presented itself, our lack of courage to witness often keeps us silent. We do not know whether we can express in a clear way what we would like to say, and we are apprehensive about the response. With practice, these feelings soon dissipate, and we become comfortable with any response (see Part I, Chapter 9, "Attitudes and Responses Encountered in Sharing Faith").

Perhaps we feel that the other person is not ready, at this point in his life, to enter into a spiritual conversation, or that we do not know him well enough to initiate one. As Rosalind Rinker says, "Maturity brings wisdom to know whether our reluctance is a lack of courage or the check of the Spirit to await God's time."[1] The more willing we are to share our faith, the more sensitive we become to timing.

Another barrier may be that we do not want to threaten the status quo of our relationship with another. We do need to be careful about this: we do not want to alienate anyone. This is where common sense, sensitivity to another's openness, and God's guidance come in.

Many Christians think that it is an invasion of privacy to speak to another on a spiritual basis. Religion is a "private matter," they say. "We don't talk about religion or politics." We have heard this so often from those who either do not have a faith to talk about or who are not aware that our Lord wants them to share it.

Many who do want to share their faith don't know how to begin talking about spiritual matters. They may feel that they need to prepare what they are to say and to contrive a conversation in which to say it. Actually, the opposite is true. To be effective, witnessing must be done in a spontaneous, sometimes almost casual manner. If you have a genuine desire to talk about your faith to another, expect God to guide you on how to begin and what to say. It is logical to expect God to guide us when we are doing something He wants us to do.

Possibly, we feel that by witnessing we may be implying that we are trying to tell another person how to live his life. But if the guidelines are followed, this won't be a problem because we will be sharing only how belonging to Christ has made a difference in our life and conduct, not preaching to him about his. When a person centers his life in Christ and trusts Him, he will seek the spiritual way to live and solve his problems, and he will receive help from God in doing so. Our witness is not for the purpose of getting him to do something, but of opening up for him new alternatives and perhaps a whole new lifestyle.

We may not want the responsibility of guiding another in the quest for spiritually based answers, expecting it to require more knowledge than we have and demand too much time and involvement. We won't be troubled by this question if we know of human and printed resources to which we can refer the person, and if we trust God to guide us in helping him.

There is one big misconception about witnessing that presents a formidable barrier—and rightly so if it were true. Many Christians think that to witness verbally for Christ they must have an aggressive personality. Images come to mind of people who go around asking, "Are you saved?" or "Are you a born-again Christian?" or "Have you received the baptism of the Holy Spirit?" as if they were asking if you have been initiated into some exclusive club. To me, this type of challenge is more a witness to the person's own ego than to Christ. This is definitely *not* what is meant by witnessing in any sense of the word as I teach it and have experienced it. One of the purposes of this book is to dissolve this image.

Another false idea about witnessing is that to witness we must be a theologian or be able to quote Scripture abundantly. However, a desire to know about theology and Scripture usually comes *after* a person knows he has faith in Christ rather than *before,* so in witnessing to a non-Christian, remember Guideline 21. In witnessing to another Christian, remember that he knows where he can learn about the Bible or theology and you can share with him books, tapes, and information about Christian education programs and renewal events.

Even if we do not feel any of these barriers, we may think we don't have anything in a spiritual way to give another. We may feel we are not good enough or advanced enough to try to guide another person in spiritual things. Although we may never become as good or advanced as we would want to, if we offer ourselves to God to be used by Him as He pleases, and if we strive continuously to learn, grow, and minister, then He will use us anyway!

Possibly we realize that God could use us to help others in this way, but we think people are not interested in spiritual discussion. When anyone tells this to Rosalind Rinker, she answers, "If so, all I can say is you don't understand people. Everyone carries some secret burden. Everyone longs for inner peace. Everyone wants a quiet heart. And everyone wants love and happiness."[2]

Robert Hall agrees: "It seems that down underneath their protective surfaces, people are hungry, hungry for the knowledge that someone cares. And if someone cares enough to share the knowledge of the power of God with them, it also tells them that Someone cares and for this they are even more hungry."[3]

This was brought home to us very forcefully some years ago when my husband and I visited a couple we had contacted through a newspaper ad to buy a filing cabinet. They asked if we needed it because we are in business. We responded by telling them that our den was floating in publications, correspondence, research notes, and other paperwork generated by our Christian ministries. The conversation then progressed spontaneously to questions of a spiritual nature: "Why aren't our prayers answered?" "How do you know God's will?" "How do you give your life to Christ?" What had been planned as a brief meeting turned into a beautiful three-hour visit in which strangers shared the things of the Lord. Ed and I told of some experiences and insights relating to those questions. As they shared their problems with us, we prayed together for each one. Within two weeks one prayer was answered. Then we followed up this "telling" witness with a "doing" witness by giving them two books which answer many of their questions and by inviting them to events where there was a witnessing ministry. What a beautiful way to acquire new friends!

# 8

# Counseling and Prayer

WHEN opportunities open to share our spiritual life with another, that encounter may involve counseling on an elementary level; it may involve praying with that person; and it *will* involve various responses. There are basic principles which will help you to handle such situations with ease.

You will always feel at peace about counseling and praying with another if you remember that God has not given you the responsibility for solving his problems. Each person is responsible for himself, and your responsibility to another is to listen and respond compassionately.

You should rarely give advice. It is better to point out alternatives if you see any, and let the person make his own choices. An outsider to the problem usually can see it more clearly than the one involved and often can suggest new ways to work it out.

Be objective. Do not get involved emotionally or otherwise entangled in the problem situation. The more embroiled you are, the less you will be capable of helping. Sympathize and give what feasible aid you can, which may include the "doing" part of being a Christian witness. If another's problem is greatly affecting your own personal life, you are too enmeshed. So take his problem seriously, but do not become too intense about it yourself.

If the problem is a financial one, do not *lend* money to the person. If you want to *give* him some, that is fine, but loaned money often has a way of never being paid back, even with the best intentions. Good relationships have been ruined because of financial involvement, and sometimes it helps the person more, in the long run, if he must work out his financial problems on his own. Seek God's guidance before you take action on another's financial needs. You may be able to help him in some other material way which will fulfill his current needs—by providing food, clothes, shelter, or by making employment or business connections for him.

If a person asks your help with a problem of any kind, you are then free to ask him personal questions, the answers to which would clarify or bear directly on the problem or its solution. A person who seeks your counsel is opening himself to you for that purpose and does not resent substantive queries into aspects of his situation which must be understood for you to respond intelligently. To the contrary, such questions make him feel you are truly interested and want to help. However, do not, out of sheer curiosity, ask questions having little bearing on the situation's solution.

Do not counsel out of your depth. If someone is emotionally or mentally ill, try to connect him with the type of help he needs. I have found witnessing of little value with these people. They simply are not able to relate to anything in a balanced way. They need professional spiritual and psychological help.

If you find yourself doing frequent counseling, it would be a good idea to read books and take courses in Christian counseling. The five day School of Pastoral Care* is the best brief but intensive experience I know for becoming a more whole person on all levels and learning to help others do the same.

Psychological understanding is a great help in counseling people, but always keep Jesus Christ central to any counseling

* The School of Pastoral Care, Inc., P.O. Box 96, Castle Rock, CO 80104.

you do. The natural and right place for Christ is at the center of our lives, working through every aspect increasingly as we grow in faith and grace; and a person's life is not whole, no matter how much psychological help he gets, if the spiritual aspect is left out. Christian psychiatrists state this point of view and so does Alcoholics Anonymous, many of whose members I have heard say that they first tried the program without the spiritual part and it would not work. (AA is non-sectarian, but its program is based on members turning over their lives to God as they understand Him.) People who seek your counsel because you witnessed to them expect and hope for a spiritually centered solution to their problems or they would not have been drawn to you by what you said.

By all means, during your private prayer time, pray for those who share problems with you. In prayer you often get insight into another person's character and problems that did not come to you during the conversation. Also, since you are witnessing, you must have experienced the power of prayer, so you will want to pray for God's direct help for the person.

If your lay ministry includes visiting hospital patients, nursing home residents, shut-ins, prisoners, or other troubled people, learn to pray aloud spontaneously when the need arises. A brief prayer which may not sound very elegant to you may have a world of meaning to the one with whom you are praying. It will also encourage him to seek God's help in prayer for himself. More than once, after saying a very simple prayer, I have had the response, "No one ever prayed for me before! That was wonderful."

Do not rely on written prayers, as beautiful as they are. You may carry a book of prayers with you and pray from it in certain situations, but more often a spontaneous prayer from the heart is the most appropriate way to pray. Be open to God's guidance about this.

When you pray with someone extemporaneously, include yourself as in need of a sense of God's presence and desirous of

His guidance so that you can identify with the person, but do not be afraid, then, to ask for the help he needs. Speak directly to God (or Jesus) in everyday language. Only include things for which the person has expressed a need for help, not ways in which *you* think he needs help! Include praise to God for His love for us. Include thanks for your friendship with the person and for anything in his situation for which thanks can be given. Close on a positive, uplifting note by thanking God that He has heard the prayer and that He is already present and active in the situation. This does not tell God what to do or claim the answer will be what we want, but it affirms what Christians believe: that God is present and active in all of life.

Avoid making statements about sin or God's will in praying with another. The purpose of the prayer is to ask God's help for him and to bring him peace. It will not be helpful—and can be damaging—to try to bring him to a conviction of sin. The Holy Spirit will convict him at the right time in the right way if he needs it. If he asks you to pray for forgiveness for him, then do it, but the request should be initiated by him, not by you. It is also unwise to make statements about God's will in praying for another, for a number of reasons. God's will is a theological issue and everyone has his own interpretation of it and of how it affects his life. More negative than positive connotations have been drawn from statements about God's will made in prayer.*

Many times, mostly in daily contacts with others, someone will mention a problem or need, but your relationship with him or the circumstances at the moment do not lend themselves to a prayer or witness. You can always say, "I'll pray for you" or "I'll remember that in my prayers." No one resents that kind of response when made in humility. I had an experience in which someone, who did not seem to have a personal relationship with God, shared with me a couple of crises in his family life and

*Recommended reading: Leslie Weatherhead, *The Will of God* (Nashville, Tenn.: Abingdon Press, 1944, 1972).

responded with genuine appreciation when I promised to pray about it. Later, when he was undergoing a crisis of his own, *he* asked *me* to pray about it.

The most interesting experiences in spontaneous prayer that I have ever heard have happened to my husband, Ed, who tells of times when he was called upon to pray on the spot:

"In my exhibits business, some time after I became a regular church member, I was working a convention in Philadelphia. One of my jobs was to be sure proper signs were placed outside the rooms in which various sessions were being held. I had to walk several blocks across town to pick up the last batch from the sign painter. I made a short cut through one of the picturesque squares with beautiful trees whose leaves had turned. Dusk was falling and the square was deserted. As I was just about through and out the other end, I heard a cry, 'Are you a man of God?' I kept walking. 'I hope he isn't calling me,' I thought. 'He must mean someone else. Besides, I don't know if I am really a man of God.' Again came the cry, 'Are you a man of God?' I stopped. Hesitatingly, I responded, 'Yes,' and began to retrace my steps. I looked all around. There were two large churches that abutted on the square, and I wondered if a clergyman in one of them could take my place. How would I respond to this person who was obviously in distress? I wished someone else were there.

"It turned out that the person calling for a man of God needed prayer. He had left his wife and children at home in New Jersey after having gone on a binge and now wanted to return to them but was afraid that he wouldn't be accepted. But I didn't know how to pray. Later in my hotel room, I realized I should have knelt in the square with him and given his whole situation to God. Instead, I said some encouraging words to him and patted him on the arm and that had to suffice.

"I soon learned how to pray extemporaneously. It's a stock-in-trade tool of practicing Christians but hardly ever acknowledged or taught by the church except as a by-product of prayer study groups. A good definition of extemporaneous prayer that I have found helpful is conversational prayer given spontaneously from the heart and applicable to the particular situation at hand.

"An excellent example of extemporaneous prayer occurred fifteen years later. I was scheduled to give a paper at a conference at Cornell University, and I needed certain information contained in a periodical located in the library at a university in Buffalo. I asked the periodical librarian for it, and she said it was the only periodical in their collection located in another building, the Law Library, on another campus. I asked her to make the proper arrangements for me to use the Law Library and when she hung up the phone, I thanked her for her help. She responded, 'I need prayer.' I asked her what was wrong, and she said her five children were giving her great travail. I asked her their ages and she responded, 'Between seventeen and twenty-nine.' I knew what the problems were, having five of my own of approximately the same ages. I said, 'I'll pray for you.' She said, 'Please not out loud.' I told her not to worry. I asked her to stand next to me in the middle of the room. There were many students in the periodical library and a great deal of milling around. No one would notice us standing together praying. They would think we were just talking. I lifted her and her children to the Lord and placed them in His hands. When we were through, I went on my way and she returned to her desk. I don't know what happened, but that's God's problem, and I know I did what He wanted me to do.

"However, a recent incident brings the power of extemporaneous prayer even more sharply into focus. A year ago in Toronto, at the annual conference of the Association for Asian Studies, about twelve of us were about ready to go out for dinner following the conference cocktail reception when a colleague came up to me and said, 'Ed, I have a problem and I've been working up my courage to talk to you about it. When you arrived at the conference two days ago, I saw you come into the hotel and it was clear to me that I should talk to you, since you had the same problem I may be facing.' We went over to a corner of the ballroom and sat down. The others went on to dinner and I told them I would join them later. As the lights dimmed and the clean-up crew swept up, my colleague laid it out. His marriage was on the rocks. He loved his wife and kids, but his wife was so unhappy with him that their relationship was miserable and this affected the children adversely. He was considering moving out of the house for the good of all concerned. We counseled together. I asked him if he had talked with his priest since he was a Roman Catholic. He said it wasn't possible because the priest had refused to get involved and had pat answers for every situation. I had been through that situation myself and understood. My first marriage had ended in divorce.

"I told him that he must not leave the house and that if a break occurred, he must do two things: level with his kids and be sure that he maintained control of his finances. I asked him if I could pray for him and he said he would appreciate that. We wrapped his family in love, asked for God's intervention, lifted up his situation and released it to the Lord. Our session together took about a half-hour, the prayer only a moment. Then he went to his other engagement and I joined my friends for dinner.

"This year the Association met in New York City, and on the first day, as I was passing through the exhibit area, I ran into my colleague. 'What happened?' I asked. 'She's coming home on Wednesday,' he responded with a smile. (It was Friday.) 'Who has the kids?' I asked. 'I do,' he replied. 'My wife is baby sitting while I am attending the conference.' He continued, 'You know, it was your prayer that activated me.' Praise the Lord, I thought, extemporaneous prayer puts Him in action in each of our lives. It works!

"I have found this to be true over the years since Philadelphia. I conduct regular prayer services, as an Episcopal lay reader, in two nursing homes and often visit with the residents after the service and pray extemporaneously with them over their problems. I also visit prisoners in a county jail, counseling and praying extemporaneously with them through the bars. This kind of prayer is also important in counseling with students when they ask for prayer or signify their need for it.

"There are eloquent prayers in the Episcopal Prayer Book that cover every situation in life in a general way, but there isn't time to pull out the Prayer Book in unstructured situations and it usually isn't appropriate. I have to pray right then to the particular situation. I send up an arrow prayer first that the Holy Spirit will give me the words or pray through me. This is not a time to worry about language, for by doing it in faith I find the Holy Spirit taking care of that.

"I find there are several steps I take naturally in almost every prayer. First, I use normal, everyday language as though I were having a conversation with the other person and with God. Second, I identify with the other person by acknowledging God's presence and my need for God's help and guidance. Third, I pray for the specific need, asking God's help for it. Fourth, I thank God that He has heard me and is already working out this problem for the highest good for the person and for God's glory.

"The results I leave to God. Often I have a feedback, as with my colleague at the Association conference. In any case, when I am finished praying, my whole being is uplifted. When I open my eyes, colors take on a brighter tinge. I feel more joyful. Extemporaneous prayer works, at least for me, and I know for others, too." [1]

# 9

# Attitudes and Responses
# Encountered in Sharing Faith

IN sharing your faith with another, it is helpful to know his mind-set, the framework in which he thinks about things, so you can know how best to approach the subject and in what terms you can speak. Try to discover his views, his interests, his family and career situation. Find ways in which you can *honestly* identify with him. Be open to his needs and try to speak to these.

If you are having a discussion with someone who is willing to talk about his spiritual life (or lack of it), you may ask such questions as, "What does Jesus Christ mean to you?" or "Do you feel that you have a personal relationship with Christ?" or "Do you believe in God?" If he says he doesn't believe in God, you might say, "What kind of God don't you believe in?" Every time I have asked that question, I always get a thoughtful, honest answer, but one which is full of misconceptions about God's nature. I then honestly reply, "I don't believe in that kind of God, either." The response, then, is to ask me what kind of God I do believe in, and we take it from there because this is a good door-opener to deeper conversation.

Give the other person an opportunity to develop and express

his thoughts, questions, doubts, prejudices, opinions, and other areas of concern so you can know, as much as possible, where he stands. Ask nonthreatening questions.

You can respond to the other person's points by sharing your own understanding of them. Such a conversation may be theological in nature, but try to illustrate your points by examples of personal experiences. He will probably remember the experiences and the points they make more easily than statements on concepts. Refrain from arguing with his views and try to stay on the positive side: what you have discovered about God's nature, reinforced by your personal experience. Your purpose is to let him know that God is alive, that He loves us, and that His love and presence make a difference.

Sometimes a person is hostile toward religion. Perhaps he has had some bad experience, either with unanswered prayer, or with the church or clergy, or with family attitudes toward church as he was growing up, or with an obnoxious person who tried to "save his soul" in one way or another. In such cases, it is usually best to say little or nothing about your spiritual life, but to give a "being" witness and a "doing" witness— to let God's love flow through you to him and help him if needs arise. If he does bring up his hostility, this is a good opportunity to agree that you might feel the same way if you were in a similar situation, and to attempt to turn his thoughts to a more positive view.

In regard to unanswered prayer, you might say something like, "I have found in my own life that God always answers my prayers, but sometimes the answer is 'wait' or 'no.'" Then you could follow by relating an experience in which you prayed for something and did not receive it right away, or at all, and it worked out for the best in another way, or God was able to sustain you through the experience. Do not try to answer the problem theologically unless the discussion develops that way.

In regard to church or clergy, you might agree that many Christians, including clergy and other church authorities, do not always live up to Christ's standards, that the attitudes or actions he deplores probably resulted from human shortcomings. Emphasize that we must look to *Jesus* as the example of what a Christian should be rather than to other Christians.

In regard to family attitudes, perhaps he was forced to attend revivals of the "hellfire and damnation" variety. You can point out that your own experience is one of a God of love and forgiveness. Perhaps he was never taken to church, and his family either ignored religion or was hostile to it. You might share your biographical witness, if you sense that he would hear you out, and bring into your witness experiences in which the church and its ministry made a difference in your life.

In regard to "soul savers," agree readily that this approach turns you off, also. You could comment that the messenger sometimes ruins the message and then share what your own faith means to you.

While talking, pray silently for the Holy Spirit to speak through you to his spiritual needs, and the right responses will come to you.

Some people are Christians in their *minds,* but not in their *hearts;* Christ is their *Savior,* but not their *Lord.* (This describes my own spiritual condition for many years.) These are among the most difficult people to whom to witness because they are under the impression that an intellectual profession of faith is the whole thing. Stories of a personal relationship to Christ, answered prayer, and other spiritual aspects of Christian living either go over their heads or threaten them.

Of course, we must never be judgmental about it, but there are many ways in which we can sense a person's spiritual condition. What is his attitude toward the spiritual life? Is he open to discussion of spiritual things, or reticent? Does he keep the discussion on an impersonal level? Does he keep changing the subject? Does he feel his life is totally committed to Christ? If so, does this commitment make a difference in his life? Does he pray privately fairly regularly? Does he feel that corporate worship is a meaningful experience? Does he read the Bible and other spiritual books frequently? Is he participating in a spiritual learning experience—a group or class? Does he tithe? Does he exercise a ministry?

It has been my experience that people whose faith is only intellectual are best reached at two different times: either when they are in crisis or when they attend a renewal event or spiritually centered group. Obviously, a person in crisis often begins to look for deeper answers and the crisis becomes the focus of his attention. A person attending a renewal event or spiritually centered group often is amazed at the whole new world which opens up to him. Encourage your priest or minister to provide opportunities for participation in small groups on a regular basis and to sponsor periodic renewal events. Groups and events of this kind are two of the most effective methods of bringing into a vital faith both nominal Christians and nonchurchgoers. There is a drawing power within a gathering of Christians talking about Christ and His relationship to them that is not always as apparent on a one-to-one basis. Small groups that have an intellectual and experiential balance also provide remarkable staying power for committed Christians. (Part II of this book is about such groups.)

You won't be able to share your faith verbally with everyone, of course. Be a good friend, a good neighbor, a good co-worker. Pray for a sense of awareness to opportunities that arise, but opportunities should never be contrived. We want people to know we like them for themselves, not because we want to "save their souls" or get them to church. Uphold them and show a genuine interest in their family, career, hobbies, etc.

When the opportunity presents itself, let people know you attend church regularly and mention other activities such as a small group or lay ministry in which you are involved. Tell them *why* you do these things and relate interesting stories that grow out of them. It is human nature to respond to an interesting story more than to a general comment. When appropriate, invite others to your church, but realize that even if they accept, they may not achieve a deepened spiritual life. "There are many people who attend church for all the wrong reasons and have never come into a living relationship with Jesus Christ," wrote Rosalind Rinker and Harry Griffith in their book *Sharing God's Love*. "Our primary objective is to help the person see that what the church is about is Christ and that what he needs is a personal relationship with Jesus."[1] There are many combinations of ways in which he can discover this and his complete response may depend in great measure on your help over a period of time.

One way to witness in a more nonverbal way is to give or lend a book that has been spiritually meaningful to you. (Best to *give* it, as books, like money, have a way of not returning!) Be sure the book will speak to the receiver on *his* level, however, which may not be the same as yours. For instance, if you are progressing deeply into a study of prayer and have read a dozen books on it, and the other person is just beginning to become interested, it is usually wiser to give him the first book you read rather than the last. The reason is that when studying something, we usually seek out more elementary books at first, then search for books on a deeper level. A book that catches a person's interest is a very effective way to create an attitude of openness, but it must be the right book, one which begins to speak to his needs. Seek God's guidance on this.

If you know another Christian whom you feel can be of spiritual help to someone, especially if he has expressed a need, try *in an uncontrived way* to get them together—perhaps at a party, or at the church coffee hour, etc.

If you have a spouse or older childen who are cool to the spiritual life, don't witness verbally to them unless they ask a direct question to which a witness is the appropriate answer. Some people leave a lot of Christian books and pamphlets around the house, hoping the spouse or children will read them. This usually won't work because they know what you are doing and it could have the reverse effect. However, your own reading placed beside your favorite chair can be a silent witness.

Ideally, parents and children should begin sharing Christian experience with one another when the children are small. There are a variety of ways to do this and it should be a continuing part of family life as long as possible. Children should be taught to pray when they are young, taking their problems to God and sharing answers with the family. There should be family prayer and Bible reading regularly. Family members should pray for one another's problems, needs and illnesses. The parents should always be open and honest with each other and with the children. Parents should let the children know of their Christian commitment and encourage them by example, instruction, and verbal sharing of spiritual things, to grow to the place where they make their own conscious commitment of their lives to Christ. Confirmation, First Communion, or whatever Christian dedication service your church provides is the ideal way to do this, as well as Baptism when administered to a mature child. Any Holy Communion service is another appropriate time to commit—and recommit—one's life to Christ, at any age. Actually, every Eucharist should be a recommitment.

Do not give your children a choice whether to attend church any more than you give them a choice whether to attend school. As long as they are in school, insist on taking them to church, and if they do not go, apply the same discipline you would if they had skipped school. As their parent, you have a right and duty to do this. By the same token, find a church with clergy, education, and activities that are spiritually centered, intellectually stimulating, and lively. You cannot blame children—or adults—for balking at meaningless, shallow, or dull Christian experiences. If you cannot find an alive church of your own denomination, consider looking elsewhere for the spiritual sustenance your family needs. You do not have to change affiliation, and you may find worship or classes meaningful in one church and small groups or youth activities meaningful in another. It is unfortunate that many Christian families must attend activities at two or three churches to find the spiritual nurture that all the members need. But the important thing is to find it.

A committed Christian family is an *ideal,* and if only one parent is a committed Christian, then he or she must do the best possible in that particular family situation. One parent may be able to accomplish only a small part of these things, but certainly that is better than no effort at all.

Even if your husband or wife does not share your spiritual life, manifest to him or her the same love and respect that you want. Depending on your spouse's character and personality, this may be easy or difficult, but spend time alone in prayer for yourself so that you will receive God's grace to live a "being" witness and use His guidance to give a "doing" witness. Invite your partner to attend worship services, renewal events, classes, or small groups with you whenever appropriate and without overdoing it. He or she should feel free to refuse and must not be asked so often that it creates an annoyance, but often enough that the spouse feels welcome. As often as possible attend events of interest to your partner, even if they are of little interest to you. Done with a cheerful attitude, such actions will show your interest in him or her as a person and partner and will encourage reciprocation.

Know that your spouse and children belong to God, whether or not they recognize this. Always keep communication open about everything. Keep a balance between your home life and your church life and ministries. Some spouses, particularly wives, spend so much time at church or in the community that they neglect their home and family relationships. This can be a big pitfall.

And—very important—pray for your family every day.

# 10

# The Dynamic of the Early Church

WITNESSING did not come out of a vacuum but developed naturally in the apostolic church, became its chief dynamic, and was one of several major lay ministries on which St. Paul structured the early Christian churches. It is encouraging to know that the witnessing we do today is the same as the witnessing they did then—the same elements, the same results, the same power which draws the Christian community into unity.

In the September 1961 issue of *Faith/At/Work,* the Reverend Claxton Monro, writing about the apostolic lay ministries he had initiated in 1954 at St. Stephen's in Houston, said, "The spiritual climate of this age makes it necessary for the witnessing ministry to be raised up, and we believe that what we are really doing is restoring to the Church the kind of approach to the Gospel that the Bible indicates was made in Apostolic times." [1]

At the 1976 convention of the Episcopal Diocese of Western New York, Richard L. Hillman, Chairman of the Commission on Lay Ministry, spoke of the need to return to the lay ministry structure of St. Paul's churches in which each member was a lay minister.

God has been telling many of us the same things—in different contexts, in different places, at different times. Today is a new age in many ways, but in terms of the spiritual condition of the world, there is *much* similarity between the apostolic era and our own day. In terms of the church, there is *little* similarity between then and now. If we learn what the dynamics of the early churches were, we can adapt them to today's churches.

Certainly, total commitment to Jesus Christ was the basis. At first, churches were no more than clusters of people who had given their hearts and lives to Him. These clusters became communities, and then churches. They had no clergy in the beginning, only the apostles traveling from city to city to instruct them, and the apostles' letters with further instruction, theological interpretation, and encouragement to submit to the Christian lifestyle.

Part of the instruction given by St. Paul in his letters concerned the definition and use of spiritual gifts and ministries, and how to structure congregational life around them. Even with Paul's education, knowledge, and wisdom, he found it necessary to refine the structure of ministries as he gained experience in directing congregations over the years. We can see this clearly in First Corinthians, written about A.D. 56, and in Ephesians, written about A.D. 62 (It is not appropriate here to discuss whether St. Paul wrote Ephesians—it certainly carries on his thinking.)

In 1 Corinthians 12:27–31 (RSV) we find: "Now you are the body of Christ and individually members of it. And God has appointed in the church first apostles, second prophets, third teachers, then workers of miracles, then healers. . . . But earnestly desire the higher gifts. . ."

In Ephesians 4:11–12 and 16 (RSV) we find: "And his gifts were that some should be apostles, some prophets, some evangelists, some pastors and teachers to equip the saints for the work of ministry, for building up the body of Christ . . . from whom the whole body, joined and knit together by every joint with which it is supplied, when each part is working properly, makes bodily growth and upbuilds itself in love."

In the apostolic church, an apostle was a person who understood the teachings of Jesus and the significance of events in His life, who had a knowledge of Scripture and a sound faith. He was intellectually and spiritually qualified to preach and to organize and maintain a constantly increasing number of committed communities of Christians. St. Paul preached, wrote guidelines, and helped organize new churches and the lay ministries upon which these churches were structured. The apostle would be the equivalent of today's bishops and other clergy.

The apostolic concept of an evangelist was quite different from the concept we have of evangelists today. Then, an evangelist was a layperson who possessed a great love for people and had a strong desire to share with them the new life of joy and peace he had found in Christ. He witnessed to them about his new life and brought them into the church where they could hear witnessing, preaching, and teaching. He encouraged them to accept spiritual disciplines which would help them discover and sustain a meaningful life with Christ. As each outsider was brought in, made a commitment to Christ, and began his spiritual journey, the evangelist would go out and bring in another. Many of today's Christians are just such quiet evangelists.

The pastor in the apostolic church was not a clergyman, but a layperson who fulfilled the role of a shepherd to the Christian community. He would take an interest in this new convert which the evangelist had brought in and help him find ways to learn, grow, and serve Christ in the church and in the world. The shepherd kept in contact with those Christians who were tempted to fall away and encouraged them to be faithful in participation. He visited the sick and the troubled. He did a lot of counseling and praying with people, as do many modern-day shepherds. Today's shepherds, also called lay ministers, lay visitors, and similar terms, do not take over the clergy's responsibilities, but supplement them.

The apostolic teacher had the same basic role in the church's life as today's teacher. He taught Scripture, doctrine, and discipline, which St. Paul regarded as vital. In his book, *Witness-*

*ing Laymen Make Living Churches,* Claxton Monro writes: ''When an individual had heard the preaching and the witnessing, if he accepted Jesus Christ as his Lord and Savior, he would then be brought to the teachers for the knowledge which Paul regarded as so highly important in the life of every Christian. We will do well to learn this lesson from the apostolic church. We get very poor results if we try to educate unbelievers into the Kingdom of God. As we let these other ministries do their work, particularly the ministry of lay witness, we will have an ever-growing group of believers who are ready and willing to receive theological content from the laymen who are qualified as teachers.''[2]

The lay ministry that St. Paul rated first in importance in both Corinthians and Ephesians was prophecy. Prophecy was the only ministry that St. Paul urged all laypersons to practice. (Other activities he advocated for everyone refer to spiritual gifts and Christian disciplines. Although St. Paul sometimes referred to ministries as gifts, the delineation between a ministry and a gift is clear: a ministry edifies the church, a gift edifies oneself unless used for ministry. Some people are more gifted at their ministries than others.) Prophecy could be practiced, whether or not the person was greatly gifted at it, because the apostolic prophet and today's prophet fulfill the same function: lay witness.*

Most people are familiar with the word *prophecy* in terms of the Old Testament prophets like Isaiah, but even scholars are vague on the definition of New Testament prophecy. For in-

---

* The first time I heard the definition of New Testament prophecy as relating to lay witness was in May 1954 by the Reverend Claxton Monro, rector of St. Stephen's Episcopal Church, Houston, Texas. As far as I know, this was the first time such an understanding of New Testament prophecy had been stated. Through the ensuing years, he has spoken about this with many theologians, clergy, and laity. In a letter to me written December 8, 1976, he said in part, ''. . . I have made no systematic list of theologians who agree, but there are many who do. . . . In St. Louis at the Episcopal General Convention (October 1964) I was startled when the visiting Roman seminarians said that they were being taught in their school that witnessing was basic to New Testament prophecy. There are some commentaries that suggest this, too.''

stance, the King James and Revised Standard versions of the Bible speak of "prophecy"; the J. B. Phillips translation calls it "speaking the word of God" and "speaking the messages of God"; the Good News Bible calls it "proclaiming God's message" and "speaking God's message"; and the Living Bible has six different explanations: "preaching the messages of God," "speaking plainly what God has revealed to me," "telling you the things I know," "telling you what is going to happen," "telling you the great truths of God's word," "preaching the deep truths of God." Others have called New Testament prophecy "exhortation" or "inspired preaching."

But if St. Paul had wanted to say that the layperson's first ministry was preaching, he would have used the word, preach. He knew that a person should be educated in theology to preach. He knew that all laypersons were not qualified to preach—in fact, very few. In his book, Claxton Monro lists statistics making it evident that prophecy was not preaching: "Some form of the word 'prophecy' appears 204 times in the New Testament. Similarly, there are 116 instances of the word 'preach.' But never does the New Testament say that a prophet 'preached' or that a preacher 'prophesies.' Furthermore, although forms of the word 'apostle' appear 80 times in the New Testament, prophecy is never mentioned as his activity. And in 6 places apostles and prophets are mentioned side by side as if they exercised different functions or offices in the church."[3]

The prophet did not teach, because this is also listed as a separate lay ministry. Although he may have done some evangelizing and shepherding in addition to his major function, he was not primarily an evangelist or shepherd because these are listed as separate lay ministries. (The apostle and teacher could witness, as they do now, but this was not as integral to their primary ministries as it was to those of the evangelist and shepherd.)

The ministry of prophecy as practiced in the apostolic church can be understood readily as witness by exploring a modern

scholar's definition of New Testament prophecy and by studying
1 Corinthians 14:1–39.

*A Theological Word Book of the Bible* defines three elements
of New Testament prophecy. It was used:

1. To announce as a revelation made by God.
2. To reveal that of which the evidence has been hidden.
3. To foretell the future.[4]

What revelation did God give to the early Christians? What
evidence had been hidden that was then revealed? How did that
make the future clear?

The answer is in the way a Christian experiences his living
relationship with his God:

1. When a person discovers that Jesus Christ is his Lord and
Savior, and he knows it in a personal, direct way—or when he
reaches a new and deeper understanding of the faith he always
has had—God has given him a revelation.

2. This truth has been hidden from him until this personal
revelation from God. Now life is different—he is different—his
understanding is enlightened. Some problems are resolved and
others take on a new perspective. Hidden sins and subconscious
emotions are being forgiven and healed. Needs are being met.
He has been helped and given a victory.

3. He foresees that if he stays on the spiritual path, he has
eternal life with Christ; that he belongs to God's people—the
Christian community, the Body of Christ; and that he has a
God-given function—a ministry in the church and in the world.

In short, the New Testament prophet was saying that God had
*revealed* to him new insights into spiritual truths and human
conditions which had been *hidden* previously from him; and that
he has experienced good results in their application; and that
this experience has led him to realize his spiritual and human
identity, led him to discover God's will for his *future* life on
earth, and led him to believe in Christ's promise of heaven.

This sounds familiar to those of us who have been involved in a situation in which someone has *witnessed* about God's action in his personal life, either privately or in a small group or large meeting or worship service. The witnesser tells about just such experiences.

In 1 Corinthians 14:1–39 (RSV)* we find a graphic account of prophecy and what it does, especially when done in the context of a gathered Christian community:

Make love your aim, and earnestly desire the spiritual gifts, especially that you may prophesy . . . . he who prophesies *speaks to men for their upbuilding and encouragement and consolation* . . . . he who prophesies *edifies the church* . . . . strive to excel in *building up the church.* . . . I want you all to prophesy. . . . Let two or three prophets speak, and let the others weigh what is said. If a revelation is made to another sitting by, let the first be silent. For you can all prophesy *one by one,* so that *all may learn and all be encouraged;* and the spirits of prophets are subject to prophets. For God is not a God of confusion *but of peace.* . . . If anyone thinks that he is a prophet . . . he should acknowledge that what I am writing to you *is a command of the Lord.* . . . So, my brethren, earnestly desire to prophesy. . . . If, therefore, the whole church assembles and . . . . if all prophesy, and *an unbeliever or outsider enters, he is convicted by all, he is called to account by all, the secrets of his heart are disclosed; and so, falling on his face, he will worship God and declare that God is really among you.*

This is exactly what happens in a modern Christian community when witnessing is done. St. Paul's language is very descriptive of what I have seen happen to countless people over the past several decades in which I have been involved in situations where there is witnessing. The speaking may or may not be done in exactly the format St. Paul describes, but a good witnessing group or service will be conducted in *peace* and *order.* A good witness will *"speak to men for their upbuilding and en-*

* Some of these verses are quoted out of order for the purpose of relating the narrative in the sequence of teaching, instruction and results. Verses are quoted in the following order: I Cor. 14:1, 3, 4, 12, 5, 29, 30, 31, 32, 33, 37, 39, 23, 24, 25.

*couragement and consolation,"* and it will *"edify the church"* and result, with the other lay ministries, in *"building up the church."* *All* present *"may learn"* and *"be encouraged"* by hearing witnesses from a number of people on a variety of subjects. When the witnesser observes these things happening, he acknowledges that what St. Paul wrote *"is a command of the Lord."* When *"an unbeliever or outsider enters, he is convicted by all"*—a conviction comes into his own heart and mind that this new life in Christ is real; that his life can be changed, his sins and mistakes can be forgiven, his unhappy memories can be healed; and that he can have a personal relationship with God now, and continuing on through eternity. No one judges him, and he doesn't tell about this conviction within himself at this point. *"He is called to account by all"*—he realizes by hearing all these witnesses that he must commit himself to this new way of life and accept the disciplines of the Christian life if he is to share in it. *"The secrets of his heart are disclosed"*—to himself: he sees his whole life in a new way, the good and the bad, and he realizes many things he never understood before. *"And so, falling on his face, he will worship God and declare that God is really among you."* After such an experience, how could he help but know that God is within this Christian community, and then worship Him?

Not only does St. Paul want Christians to witness individually in the world, as the evangelist does, and as we all can, but the witnessing about which he goes into such graphic detail is that which apparently is done in a regular church service: "If, therefore, the whole church assembles and . . . if all prophesy. . . ." The church he describes is a prophesying, a *witnessing,* community! That this ministry, practiced by all the church members, is done in the worship service is further evidenced by the mention of hymns, lessons, and other elements of worship in verse 26, immediately following his description of what happens to "outsiders or unbelievers" when they enter such a service.

From an understanding of the three elements of prophecy and

these scripture passages in light of today's witnessing experiences, it is obvious that what the New Testament calls a prophecy we today call a witness. There are other references to prophecy as witness in other books of the New Testament:

Revelation 19:10 (RSV): " '. . . I am a fellow servant with you and your brethren who hold the testimony of Jesus. . . .' For the testimony of Jesus is the spirit of prophecy."

Acts 10:42–44 (RSV): " 'And he commanded us to preach . . . and to testify. . . . To him all the prophets bear witness that every one who believes in him receives forgiveness of sins through his name.' While Peter was saying this, the Holy Spirit fell on all who heard the word." The witnessing they had been hearing opened their hearts to the preaching afterwards, converting this audience.

There are more references to verbal witnessing:

Mark 5:19–20 (TLB) (where Jesus had healed a man either insane or demon possessed): ". . . 'Go home to your friends,' Jesus told him, 'and tell them what wonderful things God has done for you; and how merciful He has been.' So the man started off to visit the Ten Towns of that region and began to tell everyone about the great things Jesus had done for him, and they were awestruck by his story."

1 Peter 3:15 (TLB): "Quietly trust yourself to Christ your Lord and if anybody asks why you believe as you do, be ready to tell him, and do it in a gentle and respectful way." That is the way all *good* witnesses are told—in a gentle and respectful way.

Acts 1:8 (RSV): "But you shall receive power when the Holy Spirit has come upon you; and you shall be my witnesses in Jerusalem and in all Judea and Samaria and to the end of the earth." I take this to refer to verbal witnessing because it refers to evangelism and because it promises that the Holy Spirit will enable Christians to witness and it is easy to discern a witness enabled by the Spirit, which all valid witnesses are.

So now we can see why the word *prophecy* in the New Testament refers less to *foretelling* and more to *forthtelling* of a person's ongoing encounter and relationship with the living Lord: how he came into his faith and his growth in faith; his guidance, answered prayers, spiritual disciplines, new insights, spiritual gifts, his healing of sin and sickness, and his ministries in the church and in the world. The Christian prophet—witnesser—is not only living on a higher level of consciousness through the Holy Spirit's power, but he is telling *how* he does it, so that pagans can be converted and Christians can be inspired, encouraged, and strengthened. This is what prophets did then, this is what they do today. So it becomes evident why, in both Corinthians and Ephesians, St. Paul lists prophecy as the *first* lay ministry and the *only* ministry which he urges *all* Christians to do.

We can see why prophecy—witness—together with the apostles' preaching and the other spiritual lay ministries, was the dynamic evangelistic force of the apostolic church. We can see why this witnessing ministry is needed again in this age, which is unlike any other age in the church except the apostolic age (the reasons for this are covered in the next chapter, "The Church's Shifting Power Focus").

We can also see why Claxton Monro said, in May 1954, "The witnessing fellowship of laymen is destined to become the focal point of power in the Church, and God is going to speak through the witnessing community in the decades ahead as He spoke through the Bible at the time of the Protestant Reformation."[5]

We who have been deeply involved in the witnessing ministry, and in the other spiritual lay ministries that go with it, have already experienced the realization of this statement. Increasingly, since the 1950s in Catholic, Anglican, and Protestant churches, these ministries have been at the heart of emerging new parish structures, and of organizations and movements in renewal and evangelism.

"What people are seeking today is a way of life which will make it possible for them to live with God and be aware of His constant Presence in their lives," said Claxton Monro.

In an age when there is great doubt about the Divinity of Jesus Christ and the inspiration of the Holy Bible, we find that the revelation of the love of God through the lives and witnesses of Christians has an effectiveness which is sometimes astonishing. . . . Our experience tells us that it is through the layman's witness in the corporate life of the Church that unbelievers will be converted, and it is through their witnessing, teaching, evangelizing and shepherding that they will come to a deeper understanding of the Lord Jesus Christ. This will make them strong, believing, serving, worshipping members of the Body of Christ.[6]

# 11

# The Church's Shifting Power Focus

T HE church has always had the essentials for community, worship, teaching, evangelism, pastoral care, and service. But in looking back over its history, even in a general way, it is evident that the church's structure and emphasis on ministries has shifted to meet the changing conditions in the world to which it ministers.

The church's drawing and sustaining power has been focused in three different ways from the beginning until the early twentieth century: the witnessing community, symbolized in the loving, close, personal relationship of the members with Christ and with each other; the institutional church, symbolized in the priesthood, sacraments, and discipline; and intellectual individualism, symbolized in the Bible, preached, studied, and personally interpreted.

During the first three hundred years, Christians believed in Christ because of what they found in His *witnesses*. They believed because of their personal encounter with Him, catalyzed and nurtured by His witnessing community. Christians won the hearts of pagans to Christ by sharing the love, joy, and peace of the Christian experience on a personal basis, both individually and corporately. It was basically an experiential Christianity— the experience of the living Lord as expressed in the community of believers. All the spiritual gifts were prevalent and all the spiritual ministries were exercised, and the apostolic church was structured on the basis of these gifts and ministries. There was so much power in this apostolic church that even the terrible persecutions could not diminish it.

The *witnessing community* was the focal point of power in the early Christian church. At that time they had no Bible as we know it. Different Christian communities had different parts of the future New Testament; some had letters from the apostles, and the Jewish Christians had the Old Testament. There was no official theology, just the teachings of the various apostles and those whom they educated, and later the bishops. Churches were not highly organized and met in homes at first.

By A.D. 313, when Constantine became emperor of the Roman Empire, these Christian communities were implanted all over the empire. They stood out because they were different. The persecutions had only strengthened them. They had a unity and a stability which the outside world did not. Christians had a purpose and goal because their lives were based on spiritual authority and moral values.

Constantine was aware of the Christian condition in the midst of his empire which was decaying in the West and chaotic in the East. Then, according to some historians, he had a Christian religious experience of his own which became a turning point in his life and in the life of the church. For whatever mixed religious and political motives he may have had, Constantine proclaimed Christianity to be the official religion of the Roman Empire. He declared Sunday as the weekly day of rest and brought together church leaders for the Council of Nicea in order to determine the official doctrine, theology, and Scripture of the Christian church. After years of prolonged squabbling over these issues, they were settled.

In the meantime, Christians became the "in crowd." Almost everyone attended church, the time requirement for Christian initiation was considerably shortened, and belief in Christ gradually came to be accepted more on the basis of the doctrine and discipline taught by the church rather than on the strength of a life-changing experience nurtured and deepened within a closely knit community.

Between the fourth and seventh centuries, the scattered Christian communities became the centralized Christian church, and there was a great shift in emphasis upon spiritual gifts, lay ministries, and church structure. By A.D. 600 Gregory I was pope, and the church was gaining both religious and political power.

Between the seventh and thirteenth centuries, Christians believed in Christ because of what they found in His *church*. The *priesthood* was the focal point of power in the church, the center of discipline, authority, and law. Spiritual gifts and ministries, for all practical purposes, ceased to exist among the laity. The church structure, consequently, was based on the structures laid down by the hierarchy, rather than on the exercise of lay ministries as in the past. The hierarchy was educated, but the majority of lay people could not even read or write. They looked to the priest for all information about theology, Scripture, sacraments, values, and personal discipline.

In the thirteenth century a new restlessness began to stir in Europe brought about by economic, political, and educational factors, resulting in a new sense of personal independence. From the thirteenth to the sixteenth century, there was another shifting period in the church, which culminated in the great upheaval of the Reformation.

From the sixteenth century on, an increasing number of Christians came to base their belief in Christ on what they found in the *Bible*. The invention of the printing press eventually made copies of the Bible available to virtually everyone, and it progressively became more central in preaching, teaching, and personal study. Christians found it enlightening and exciting to learn about Christ directly from the Bible—like a new revelation of God to His people. So the *Bible* became the focal point of power in the church. Protestant churches even placed the pulpit in the center of the sanctuary, replacing the altar, thus symbolizing that the Bible was the new center of authority in the church. Many backsliding Christians and unbelievers were won to a zealous faith through preaching and teaching based on the authority of the Scriptures.

Bible preaching has been the center of evangelistic practice down through the nineteenth and early twentieth century—campaigns, crusades, missions, revivals, etc.—to such an extent that Bible preaching and evangelism have become synonymous in most people's minds. But in the latter half of this century all that is changing as, again, a new restlessness emerges in the Christian church—both Catholic and Protestant. Not that the Bible isn't a central element in our faith—it is still God's book and one of the basic elements upon which our faith is based and nurtured. But there are people all around us (many in the pews!) who cannot be reached for Christ by conventional methods. They don't believe Jesus is the savior of the world. Many believe religion is outmoded or is superstition or their spiritual search has led them to cults, Eastern religions, or to the occult. They don't believe that the Bible is God's book, so at the outset this argument is based on an assumption which does not exist for them. They believe that other great books are just as inspired. They don't believe that the institutional church is God's representative on earth, so they don't accord any divine authority to it. All of the politics and the internal squabbling in the church (frequently making headlines) just supports their cynicism.

Today many people think of the early church as simply history, as events that happened long ago and far away to people who were different and who lived in quite another world. But those of us who have been ministering within the heart of any aspect of the great renewal movement, which began in a small way in the 1920s and whose momentum has since affected millions of lives throughout the world, see another picture.

We realize that we too are living in a pagan society, ministering to people of like mind to those in the world of the apostolic church. They had many gods, our society has many gods. They were seeking many transitory pleasures, so is our society. Their serious thinkers were devising new philosophies of life as they sought to enrich temporal life with eternal meanings, so are ours. Although they did not have generations of Christianity behind them, as our society has, still, to a very great extent, our society lives and thinks as if it had never heard of Jesus Christ.

The Christian church in this century, with the exception of the World War II period, has largely failed to reach the outside world or even to make the gospel relevant to its own. The decreasing number of active members, the combining of congregations, the closing of churches—all attest to this. All mainstream churches—Protestant, Anglican, and Catholic—share these experiences in common.

The church is again in a great shifting period, this time returning to the Christian witnessing community structure, rediscovering Paul's ministries, and manifesting spiritual gifts. Parishes today which are apostolic-type witnessing communities are those whose clergy preach the centrality of a personal relationship with Christ and a loving relationship with one another. They train lay people in witnessing, evangelism, shepherding, and teaching ministries. They launch small groups for study, prayer, and sharing, and support members in outreach ministries and services. These parishes are thriving because they are expressing the kind of life and exercising the kinds of ministries, within and outside of the church, that are effective and meaningful in today's world.

Today's pagans are responding to this Christian lifestyle as yesterday's pagans did. Today's Christian church can have the same impact on society as yesterday's had.

God is making very clear the direction in which He is leading the church. How exciting it is to live, love, worship, witness, and minister upon the crest of its growing edge!

*Part Two*

# Christian Small Groups

**OR HOW TO PARTICIPATE IN A SMALL GROUP
WITHOUT BEING OFFENDED**

# 1

# A Learning Situation,
# Not a Teaching Situation

C HRISTIAN groups are for people who accept the Christian faith as an unfolding way of life—changing, deepening, developing—and for those who want to discover spiritual reality but who are still groping, and for all who are ready to apply personal religious experience to their wider social, business, or political activities,'' wrote Irving Harris, Presbyterian layman, author, and founder of the Faith/At/Work organization and magazine. ''To see, to pray, to grow, to share and to apply—these are the verbs at the heart of the Christian cells.''[1]

Emphasizing the necessity of the relationship of small groups to the church, he continued, ''Even the group in which conversions take place, and where individuals find it possible to become vocal about what God has done for them—even such a fellowship falls short of the mark unless it forms an organic part of the Body of Christ, the Church. Groups per se are not an answer, nor an end in themselves. God's love and life, as mediated in Jesus Christ, are the heart's deepest desire, and the need of the Church and the world.''[2]

When a small group is an integral part of the church's ministry, and it is based on the premise that Christ is Lord and Savior, it functions in a manner that dispels the common apprehensions people have about belonging to a group. As with witnessing, negative scenes often come to mind about small groups. Thoughts of humanistic encounter groups, as depicted in films and magazines, convey a situation in which everyone is challenged—usually in a very offensive way—to reveal his inmost feelings and secret sins. But such groups are *not* the type that Irving Harris wrote about nor those that are the subject of this book.

Even if a person realizes that a Christian small group is not like that, he may fear he will be offended by listening to others share experiences he considers too personal to talk about. But in a properly conducted group this does not occur.

Another reason some Christians avoid small group participation is that they feel that they do not know enough about their faith or the Bible for such a discussion. They feel comfortable in a class where they are taught, but they realize that a group situation is different, and they fear that they may be embarrassed because of their ''ignorance.'' Actually, the small group experience would be most helpful to such persons.

There are many different kinds of small groups with varied purposes. The basic types of groups defined here are the ones about which Irving Harris wrote. These groups have meant the most to the greatest number of people through the years because they are easy to start and easy to conduct, because they are more involved with the spiritual than the psychological, and because they do not depend on teachers or highly trained leaders (although some training is certainly desirable and is necessary for the avoidance of pitfalls). Through such groups we do mature psychologically, but the basis of that growing maturity is spiritual.

Most of us assume that learning requires a human teacher, just as most of us assume that ministry requires ordination. But just as there are many kinds of ministry and ways to minister, there are many methods of learning and ways to learn.

From my personal Bible study, I see three ways of learning emphasized. First, we learn from a human teacher: St. Paul always lists teaching as one of the most important lay ministries. Second, we learn from others in a group context: there are numerous references to ways in which the early Christians learned from one another while gathered for worship and the exercise of various spiritual gifts and ministries. Third, we learn from God directly through study, prayer, and experience. I have found three places in the New Testament and one in the Old Testament which say that God Himself will teach us and that we do not need a human teacher:

1 John 2:27 (GNB): "But as for you, Christ has poured out His Spirit on you. As long as His Spirit remains in you, you do not need anyone to teach you. For His Spirit teaches you about everything, and what He teaches is true, not false. Obey the Spirit's teaching then, and remain in union with Christ."

John 6:45 (RSV): "It is written in the prophets, And they shall all be taught by God.' Everyone who has heard and learned from the Father comes to me."

1 Thessalonians 4:9 (RSV): "But concerning love of the brethren, you have no need to have anyone write to you, for you yourselves have been taught by God to love one another."

Isaiah 54:13 (RSV): "All your sons shall be taught by the Lord . . ."

I do not see these three methods of learning as contradictory, but as complementary! What this says to me is that for spiritual growth and understanding, learning from a human teacher is indispensable, learning from others is indispensable, and learning directly from God Himself is indispensable.

In Christian small groups there is no human teacher. If you have a small group with a teacher, you have in actuality a small *class,* even if you include discussion. This is a very effective type of educational situation because you usually can learn more in a small class than in a large one, but this is not a small group in the sense that this book defines it.

Yet, a small group is a learning situation in that the members share what God is teaching them directly through study, prayer, and experience, and they share how these insights are working out in their own personal lives. The members are not teaching each other in a formal way because they are not relating explicit theological concepts. But what they say will, at times, contain implicit theology, the acceptance and application of which is self-initiated within the other participants rather than taught to them as truth they should believe and use. They learn from each other through that which is expressed and accepted in the context of the group experience and applied in their daily lives. One who learns in experiential processes is validly taught, as is he who learns from a teacher doing formal teaching.

Although a small group does not have a teacher, it does have one or more leaders, but they function more as facilitators or guides. (Their responsibilities are outlined in Part II, Chapter 15, "Leadership Responsibilities.")

# 2

# Elements, Purposes and Composition of Christian Small Groups

C HRISTIAN small groups, like witnessing, developed in the early church as a natural heritage from Jewish tradition. "The small community or fellowship of Christians has an honorable lineage," wrote Helen Shoemaker in her manual, *Schools of Prayer for Leaders and Learners:*

It is the descendant of the informal fellowship of the ancient Jews. In the mists of history, small groups of Jews met on the Sabbath Eve for supper and prayer. Each small group was called a Chabburah. Jesus and His disciples, most probably, formed such a company with bonds of love and mutual commitment. The early Christian Church, growing out of the experiences of the Jewish community, included both the Ecclesia and the Agape. The Ecclesia was the organized church worship centered in Holy Communion. The Agape was its Chabburah, where the informal fellowship of those who loved one another in Christ took place. In the company of a small close group, Jesus revealed Himself most fully.[1]

Speaking of today, the Anglican bishop, Stephen Neill, says, "The gospel must be brought back to where people live, in simple forms, and in terms of small and manageable fellowships."[2]

I call such a fellowship a "Christian small group" to differentiate it from any other kind of small group with purposes and functions not grounded in the Lordship of Christ. Christian groups and humanistic groups may have some elements in common, but all groups written about here are Christian groups.

I define a Christian small group as one in which up to a dozen people meet together regularly, either for a specified or unspecified number of sessions, for one, some, or all of the following purposes: (1) study of a book; (2) silent and audible spontaneous prayer; (3) verbal witnessing and sharing of insights; (4) meditation; (5) singing and praising; (6) introspective and interpersonal relating. These six basic elements of small group experience may be mixed and matched in any way or only one element may be chosen as the group's sole activity.

Each element serves its own purpose: (1) to learn more about the Bible, faith, prayer, healing, spirituality, and living the Christian life; (2) to practice prayer more effectively and to channel prayer power to others for mental, physical, and spiritual healing; (3) to tell and to hear what God is doing in one another's daily life and to share new insights learned as a result of personal prayer, study, and experience; (4) to learn how to communicate with God on a deeper level; (5) to share in unstructured praise and spontaneous song; (6) to know and understand oneself and others better and to help them do the same.

The results of participation in such groups are as diverse as the people themselves. As you will see, not all of these elements are suited to everyone. However, those participants who have discovered a group which is meaningful for them experience deep and lasting benefits. They learn more about themselves, God's nature, and spiritual principles. They grow in awareness of what God expects of them and what they can expect of Him. They learn how to minister spiritually to one another and develop ministries which they carry into the community. They encourage one another to keep the disciplines necessary for spiritual growth. They mature in prayer. They become united with the other group members in a strong bond of love—*agape*—which spills over into their entire lives and pervades their other relationships.

Small groups may be composed of a general mixture of people or of people in certain categories or circumstances. Groups may be created for people with a common problem or with interest in a particular subject. Successful groups exist for men, women, and youth; singles, couples, and persons widowed or divorced; businessmen, businesswomen, housewives, and the unemployed; recovered alcoholics and drug addicts; former mental patients and those with emotional problems; prisoners and parolees, etc. A group's goals and purposes depend on the people who comprise it and what their needs and desires are.

Experience has demonstrated an interesting fact, and this is that Christians and searchers cannot be mixed in the same group for it to fulfill its functions to either. Such a group will soon fall apart because all or most of the elements comprising a Christian group are based on theological assumptions that as yet have not been accepted—and perhaps not even explored—by the searcher.

Searchers are those who are agnostic, or who believe in a creative force but not in a personal God, or who have been following another religion. In essence, as far as Christianity goes, they are unbelievers, but I call them searchers because they would not attend a Christian worship service or class or small group if they were not at least somewhat open-minded and were not looking for something beyond their present understanding.

It is obvious that the mind-set and the spiritual needs of searchers and committed Christians are very different. Of course, there are individuals who will be exceptions to any rule, and a certain searcher may join a group of committed Christians, adopt their disciplines, and discover a personal relationship with Christ. But where this happens, the searcher is usually the *only* searcher in a group of Christians and is usually already intent on discovering a Christian identity. A Christian joining a group of searchers, on the other hand, will soon become bored (unless he feels called to an evangelism ministry) because he needs spiritual "meat" and a searchers' group, of necessity, provides only spiritual "milk."

The only successful groups I know of that serve both Christians and searchers are to be found in the marketplace (see Part II, Chapter 17).

Groups for searchers have an evangelistic purpose and should be so geared. The methods, formats, and techniques of this type of group are, for the most part, quite different from those of groups for Christians, and we will touch on these in other chapters. Groups for searchers need to be part of the structure of a comprehensive evangelism program within a parish or within a ministering organization. Such groups formed as a separate entity will have a difficult time surviving.

The bulk of Part II of this book is on groups for committed Christians because most small groups meeting in churches and homes are geared to their needs, emphasizing spiritual and emotional growth, ministry within the group, and a life structured on Christian disciplines. These groups touch our personal lives and relationships and catalyze our ministries in the church and in the world.

# 3

# A Group by Any Other Name…

TO describe the myriad variety of small group structures and functions would fill several books, but to
name each group is an even more complex task because groups
with the same name rarely do the same things!

The most common example of this is the term *prayer group,*
which is loosely applied to many different kinds of groups
whether or not they do much praying! To me, a prayer group
may study a book, and may even have a short discussion, but
the main function of a prayer group is to *pray,* and a true prayer
group will spend most or all of its time in prayer. But I have attended so-called prayer groups where there was very little
prayer. They were mostly study, discussion, and witnessing
groups. I have even attended a group in which each week a different member read for an hour anything she felt was inspira-
tional—meditations, poems, book chapters, stories from church
bulletins—and closed by reading some printed prayers; and that
was called a prayer group!

Another term, *house church,* has become an umbrella covering widely divergent groups. That term as I first heard it, back
in the mid-1950s in my Houston parish, was applied to weekly
open evangelistic meetings in homes, to which searchers were
brought to hear a man and a woman witness. This was followed

by a brief discussion and refreshments. Another form of meeting evolved which added singing and scripture reading, and it became a group with the combined purposes of evangelism and spiritual feeding for new Christians. It also was called "house church."

Today, in St. John's–Grace Episcopal Church, Buffalo, we have closed home meetings for church members who are committed Christians, in which eight to twelve people agree to meet for a certain number of weeks to study a book, listen to tapes, have discussions in depth, and pray for one another—and they call these "house churches"! Frankly, this current house church is more like the weekly Faith Study and Prayer Fellowship groups I used to attend in Houston, except the number of meetings was open-ended.

Friends here and in Canada tell me of an entirely different kind of group called "house church," which is actually a church meeting in a house. Its members "covenant" to become a Christian community, holding their worship, education classes, small groups, and other activities in a home. Members may or may not be all of one denomination. They may have an ordained minister who participates for little or no pay. All the money collected is used entirely for lay ministry outside the "house church."

You can begin to see the impossibility of defining small groups by title. Perhaps you have heard other titles such as Share and Care, Prayer and Praise, Cottage Meeting, Intercession Group, Healing Group, Witnessing Group, Sharing Group, Meditation Group, Talk-It-Over Group, Fellowship Group, Christian Cell, and Extended Family. These groups are also spiritually centered, but cannot be described by title, either.

On the other hand, there are such groups as Serendipity, Transactional Analysis, Sensitivity, Encounter, Values Clarification, Awareness Development, etc., which have specific structures and functions that apply to a unique type of activity developed under that name, so that their titles do refer only to those groups. The concepts of such groups are not related to the spiritual life except insofar as an individual member applies personal spiritual values to them, but they can be conducted with a Christian orientation.

In referring to different types of Christian small groups, I use the term *prayer group* for one whose basic function is prayer; *study group* for one whose basic function is study; *witnessing group* for one whose basic function is witnessing, etc., even though they may contain other elements. However, I do not base description of groups on *titles* but on *elements* because creating a small group involves selection of elements, and you can create a group that will perform one function or several, and each function requires different elements.

In choosing elements for your small group, base your choices on people, purposes, and circumstances. You also must decide in what form you will use each element. After your group has been meeting for awhile, there can be a shift in emphasis, which may come about gradually as some elements are needed more than others, or as a different form of an element emerges through group experience. Reasons for this can range from personal preference to spiritual growth. Be open to God's guidance about this. You can expect God to guide the group He calls together.

# 4

# Element One—Study of a Book

**M**OST small groups meet for the basic purpose of studying the Bible or other books. These groups frequently have two other elements—prayer and witnessing—but to a lesser degree than study, since often the prayer and witnessing just naturally develop as members know one another better and begin to share experiences. Participants who want these three elements from the group's inception divide the time in thirds to include adequate opportunity for each.

If you study the Bible, use modern translations and stick to the New Testament. Members should choose whichever translation they like best, even the King James Version if that is their preference, but generally modern translations are easier to understand, provide varied shades of meaning, and are therefore easier to relate to one's own experience. Older people feel more comfortable with the King James Version as a rule, but it is important to use more than one version.

The New Testament is a Christian's guideline for faith, for an understanding of God's nature in the Trinity, and for application to daily living. The Old Testament, on the other hand, is best studied privately or in a class with a qualified teacher in order to acquire an understanding of the historical background for Christianity and of the development of man's concepts of God. Both

Old and New Testaments are good for the discussion of concepts, but the New Testament is also good for experiential relating which is more difficult to do with most of the Old Testament. The purpose of small group Bible study is not, basically, to formulate abstract intellectual concepts, or to learn facts about the history, social conditions, and customs of the day, or to understand the developing concepts of God's nature through the ages. All of these aspects are part of any Bible study, but *emphasis* on them is best left to Bible *classes*.

Although theory is the basis of practice, the main purpose of small group Bible or book study is more practice than theory. The emphasis here is on learning how to apply Christian concepts in daily life, how to receive God's grace, how to deepen one's own faith, how to mature in prayer, how to use spiritual gifts, and how to exercise ministries—as well as on sharing experiences growing out of doing what the group is learning.

In reading the group assignment, three basic questions will serve as guideposts: (1) What does this tell me about God? His nature? His will? His methods? (2) What does this tell me about myself? My attitudes? My lifestyle? My current situations? (3) What does this tell me to do? Is there an instruction to be obeyed? A promise to claim?

Before studying the designated Scripture reading, which should be done prior to the meeting, the group member should pray that God will reveal insights into the Scripture's meaning and the way in which the principles illustrated affect his own life. This is how I study, so I know it works. In the group, discussion should center on these insights and their personal applications. This is where witnessing comes into the group naturally.

The beauty of this approach is that the participant, through Bible study, not only receives God's direct teaching to himself, but he receives God's direct teaching to every other member of the group through their sharing. This, to me, is the main value of belonging to a study group. If you study the Bible privately, you have one teaching; if you go to Bible class, you have another teaching; if you attend a study group, you have many other teachings.

As you grow in spiritual maturity and understanding, the quality of your insights deepens and you are able to apply them more effectively in your daily life. You help others on a progressively deeper level by sharing, and other maturing members help you. This is why it is a good idea to try to participate in some kind of study group on a regular basis throughout life.

Many groups study other books dealing with faith, prayer, or healing, Christian living and Christian discipline, the meaning of commitment, spiritual ministry to others, understanding oneself, and many other topics. There are some old classics in these fields that will never be surpassed, and there are many good new books coming out constantly. Some groups study only the Bible, some only other books, some switch back and forth. The group should study what the majority feels a need for. If they stay together for a long period of time, they will find they need different emphases at different stages of their development. I think this is healthy.

Group members should never feel guilty if they want to study something other than the Bible. The change is good. Learning in depth from an author's insights and experiences in one subject is, I have found, indispensable to spiritual growth and understanding. In my experience, those people have been proven wrong who say, "Study only the Bible because it is God's word and books are only human interpretations. You should get it straight from the Lord." As far as I am concerned, many authors I have read have gotten it "straight from the Lord," and in a more understandable and in-depth manner than I could ever get it from the Bible. But it is not either/or; it is both/and. It is best to balance your reading as much as possible.

Some books have special techniques for study—accompanying guides, cassettes, projects, written work—and it is beneficial to study them in the designated ways. The majority do not, and they should be studied in the same way as the Bible: praying for God's enlightenment and keeping in mind the three questions.

Regarding use of Bible commentaries and other references in group study, I have found both advantages and disadvantages. It is good to have the added understanding of the facts, circumstances, geography, and social and political conditions of the day. On the other hand, we often tend to get bogged down in the factual approach when we use such material. The purpose of group study, remember, is to discover more about our personal relationship to God and His to us, and how this works out in daily life, not solely to share facts or concepts. But because most people are of the view that a Bible or book discussion is historical or conceptual in nature, and because they are not used to an experiential approach, it is too easy to carry on the discussion only on an intellectual level, and too difficult to move into the application. Reference material, when used in the discussion, tends to reinforce this approach.

If you want to use a commentary, do this at home and do not bring it to the group. Use the commentary only for better understanding of the background of the text, and do not let it take the place of what you are to learn from God about personal relationship and direction for your life. However, in a Bible *class,* commentaries are very helpful because they can elucidate the type of subject matter being taught.

Study guides such as those published by The Bible Reading Fellowship* are excellent for group use because they incorporate pertinent discussion questions—involving both the conceptual and experiential aspects—and they offer a comprehensive program for both personal and group study using the Bible, good books, and cassettes. In my opinion, the BRF has the outstanding program in its field.

Regarding the mechanics of group Bible or book study, there

---

* The Bible Reading Fellowship, P.O. Box M, Winter Park, Florida 32790.

are several ways this can be done, and either the leader or members may determine this.

One way is to have each member take his turn sharing what he wishes without interruption or comment from others until everyone has had an opportunity to share (or to pass). Time allotment can be controlled best this way, and a limit may be imposed on each person or on this segment of the group's activity. When all have shared their insights, there may be open response. The advantage of this procedure is that every member gets an opportunity to share. A disadvantage is that good discussion points may be lost in response time unless notes are made, which creates a more formal tone.

Another way is to take turns but allow response after each person speaks. The advantage to this is that group discussion tends to be more informal and more discussion results. The only disadvantage is that in some groups the person speaking may be interrupted by responses and ensuing discussion, and with this happening to every member, it is difficult to control the time.

The most informal way of sharing is just to let everyone speak as desired, with spontaneous response. This method usually works best in a very small group whose members have been meeting awhile and know each other well. There is enough time with fewer people and no one will feel reticent about speaking or try to dominate the discussion, since they all feel accepted and an integral part of the group. The advantage of this method is complete spontaneity, which leads easily to in-depth sharing of insights and experiences and frequently results in the most benefits to everyone. I personally prefer it. A disadvantage of using this method in a larger group can be that not everyone will be able to share, especially if there are some talkative members and some shy members.

Whichever way is chosen, the assigned material should always be read in advance, not in the group. Some groups take a chapter, especially of the Bible, and each member takes turns reading. To me, this is boring and a waste of time. It seems reminiscent of first-grade reading exercises. Discussion may take place as they read or following the complete reading, but this method tends to create a more stilted response and one that focuses on history or theology. The greatest disadvantage to this method is that it encourages members not to bother reading the material ahead of time and, therefore, since they have not studied it and meditated on it, they have no new insights to share. If the members do read it ahead anyway, then reading aloud in the group is superfluous.

To some of you who have never participated in a study group, this kind of study may sound as if we are "pooling our ignorance," as someone said to me who apparently had never experienced such a group. However, after years of active participation in many group experiences, I can assure you that it is anything but this. It is a *vital* and *lively* way of learning.

# 5

# Element Two—Silent and Audible Spontaneous Prayer

**P**RAYER is an essential element in any Christian small group experience for many reasons. Whatever the purposes of a group, prayer is the cohesive factor. Prayer is a channel for God's love and human love. Prayer is a uniting force between people. Through prayer comes guidance for problems and new ideas for creativity. Prayer is a power that accomplishes much, sometimes in unusual and surprising ways. Many pray-ers multiply that power. Prayer may be only one of several elements in a small group, or it may be the main or only element—in which case it is truly a "prayer group." Either way, prayer in a small group is one of the most supportive elements in the lives of its members. This dynamic cannot be explained; it must be experienced.

In liturgical churches, we are accustomed to using written prayers composed by others, both in church and in private devotions. It is fine to use such prayers, and at such times we usually offer our own silent prayers in addition. In a small group, however, the use of written prayers should be limited so that members' prayers will be personal and specific.

The suggestions given for praying with another person in Part I, Chapter 8, may be applied in group prayer.

When you pray in small groups, as when alone, you are talking to God from your heart. Prayer is not telling others what you are going to talk to God about or what you want Him to do. I have heard people say during prayer times, "Let's ask for God's help for John who is in the hospital for surgery." And that is their prayer! They are suggesting that we ask God's help for John, but they themselves are not asking His help at that moment. Instead, speak directly to God—something like, "Lord, help John feel close to you while he is in the hospital, take away all fear of pain, guide the doctors and nurses and others as they minister to him, and let your healing power work in him for his complete recovery. Thank you in Jesus' name. Amen." You don't need to use those exact words, of course—use your own. That is prayer from the heart.

Another prayer habit which needs changing is the use of the phrase, "Be with John." I hear almost everyone include such a petition. But we don't need to ask God to be with anyone. He is with everyone at all times, whether they and we know it or not. I always think it is rather insulting to God to ask Him to do what He is already doing, what is actually His nature. So I pray something like, "Help John to sense your presence," or "Help John to know you're with him."

Remember that you are not praying for the approval of other group members. This is a pitfall for many when they first start praying aloud in groups. They pray more *for* other people than *to* God, although they don't mean to. It is a natural result of the self-consciousness in doing a new thing. Practice is the only remedy for this. Also, you can ask God in your private devotions to enable you to pray better spontaneously. He will!

Learn to pray as if you were talking to someone with whom you have a personal relationship, because you *are*—you have a personal relationship with God, Christ, the Holy Spirit—and your relationship will grow and deepen in a small group, and you will find spontaneous prayer easier as you go along.

Some people want to know why it isn't as good to pray

silently as it is to pray aloud in a group. For one thing, you learn how to express yourself in prayer better when you can pray aloud as easily as silently. For another—the more important reason for me—when you pray aloud, others pray silently along with you, praying what you are praying, and all minds, hearts, and souls are united in this one prayer, multiplying its power and effectiveness; and this is why you pray for some need: for power and effectiveness. Pray loud enough for the group to hear you. Some timid members mumble so softly that it is impossible to join with them.

You may, however, pray silently together by mentioning each name for intercession and then allowing a period of silence for each one to pray, in his own way, for that person. There is nothing wrong with this method if it isn't a way to avoid audible prayer. Group members should learn to do either with equal ease. There are times when one or the other type of prayer seems more appropriate. Let the Holy Spirit guide.

Never try to force a person to pray aloud. People who have never experienced small group prayer will need time to get used to the idea and to learn by listening to the leader and others pray aloud. After people have been in the group awhile, if they still don't pray aloud, the leader should gently encourage them to do so, but never put them "on the spot."

Group members may take turns praying, either in order or as they feel a desire to do so. If in order, the person who doesn't want to pray may simply say "Amen" or recite a Scripture verse to indicate that the next person may take his turn. Prayer may be done at the beginning and at the end of a meeting. Prayers at the beginning should not be petitions or intercessions, but acknowledgment of God's presence, request for His blessing, thanksgiving for answered prayer, etc. Often only the leader offers an opening prayer. Closing prayers may be thanksgiving, petition, intercession, etc. The reasons that petitions and intercessions are saved until the end are: (1) the group consciousness is united and on a higher spiritual level at the end rather than the start when people have perhaps rushed in, have their minds on the day's events, and have not "settled in" yet; (2) needs are often expressed during the meeting that should be prayed for; (3) prayers answered since previous sessions will be mentioned during the meeting as conversation brings them to mind, so petitions turn into thanksgivings.

The person who expresses a need or makes a prayer request for another may not, necessarily, be the one to say the prayer. Also, any need can be prayed for by more than one person. There are no rules about this. The leader should make certain, however, that every request and every need expressed is remembered in prayer, at least once, before the meeting ends.

The mechanics of the prayer time should be conducive to making the members feel comfortable. I personally prefer to sit rather than to stand. For some reason, I concentrate better when sitting. During a meeting I sometimes make notes about prayers I want to say at the close, and the notes can just rest on my lap during prayer if we are seated. A gesture which makes some feel uncomfortable is that of holding hands around the circle while in prayer. Women especially are prone to do this, but many mixed and men's groups do, also. If the group members feel close to one another, and they *all* want to hold hands in prayer, then it is a meaningful way to pray. But if it is the idea of only a few, and the leader has never asked how everyone feels about it, then it should not be done until everyone agrees. Since people want to be friendly and go along with their group, they are likely to acquiesce without complaint when several hands go out, even though it goes against the grain. Even a friendly touch such as this is a personal thing and should not be forced.

If the members keep a prayer list, it should be updated at each session. As prayers are answered and crossed off the list, it is encouraging to see evidence that God answers prayer for every kind of need, and it is a real thrill to know that God has used us as channels for His power. Not every group keeps a prayer list, or should. Again, it depends on the purposes of the group. Most women's groups do, and, frankly, women do much better in this area than men.

A warning about prayer lists: they can be great, but their misuse has caused more problems than anything except problem people! Here are some hard and fast rules all groups should make for prayer lists:

1. Be sure every member of the group really wants to maintain a prayer list for the purpose of praying privately, and preferably daily, for those on the list. If the members don't really want to, they won't get around to it, even if they agree to it out of duty. And if they do it out of duty instead of desire, how effective would it be?

2. Put every member of your group on the list. As different members express various concerns, pray for those when you pray for that member.

3. *Keep the list short. This is the most important rule.* Letting the list grow too long causes problems. For some reason, many groups have a big problem about limiting their prayer list. Every member of the group has a spouse or children or relatives or friends and friends of friends—or even has seen a news story about someone who needs prayer—and they add all the names to their group list as if by magic all the needs will be met if only the names are on the list. Often names are left on for months, maybe longer, when no one knows what has become of the person. Often requests are for problems or illnesses that would take a miracle to solve or to heal. Those people deserve to have a real, concentrated prayer sent their way, not just a quick mention of their names among dozens of others!

I once had sixty people on my prayer list whom I was supposed to pray for daily. I finally split up the list into seven parts and prayed for some each day. Now I no longer allow my list to grow that long. Recently, a woman from a local church lamented to me that her group had accumulated over one hundred names for whom they were supposed to pray daily, and they were at their wit's end trying to fulfill what they thought was their "obligation"! Their rector asked them (and rightly so) "Why don't you just open the phone book and start praying?" I told her that I had gotten out of that trap, and that she should, too!

The cause of this problem, as I see it, is false guilt brought on by a misguided sense of responsibility to pray for everyone who asks. Members of groups especially fall victim to this since they receive many requests from people who know they are in a group (perhaps these people should be in their own group?). Many feel guilty, also, if they hear, second-hand, of a big need and don't add it to their group's list.

I tell these group members not to feel guilty. No one person can be responsible for making sure everyone in the world is prayed for. In fact, Agnes Sanford, author of many books on prayer and spiritual healing and founder of the School of Pastoral Care, tells us to pray only for those people "in your bundle." She says that the Spirit draws you to pray for certain people with whom you have a spiritual affinity, and these are the ones God wants you to pray for. You may pray for others and be a channel for help, but you are *responsible* only for the ones "in your bundle."

Here are rules for keeping the prayer list short:

1. Pray on a regular basis for a private list of those for whom you feel a real concern. Whenever anyone asks you for prayer and you don't want to put him on your list or your group's list, pray once for him and release him to God's care, thanking God that He is helping him. You may also pray for him during the group's intercession time.

2. Set a limit of *one* name (or at most *two* if the group is small) that each member may put on the prayer list. If a member wants more than this, he may change the names as often as desired. By the same token, he may leave one name on indefinitely. *Stick to the limit. No exceptions.*

3. A member may pray for as many people as he wishes

(within reason) during the intercession time, so that no one for whom a member is truly concerned need go unprayed for by the group. But neither is the group burdened unnecessarily by long daily prayer lists.

4. If members request daily prayer for their immediate families, perhaps that should be their allotment for the list: some people have large families! You may need to pray for them as a family unit rather than individually. Let common sense rule.

A word about prayer chains. This can be a very effective method of summoning prayer in an emergency, but again, this should be done only if the group members truly want it. At times a member or his loved one will receive bad news, or find himself in a crisis, or experience sudden illness, or have an accident, and desire prayer. Some groups have a prayer chain arrangement whereby each member keeps a list of members' names and phone numbers at home and at work. When one receives a call, he calls the next on his list (if that one can't be reached, he calls the next) and that person then calls the next on his list, etc. Within a few minutes a lot of people can be praying, and many attest to the effectiveness of such prayers. It is not necessary to belong to a group to be involved in a prayer chain, however. A suburban Buffalo church operates such a chain by publishing one person's number, who then starts the chain. All the parishioners are invited to join periodically and are free to stop at any time.

The true "prayer group" or "intercession group," which meets for prayer alone or which spends half its session in prayer and half studying prayer, carries special conditions in order for it to be what it is.

Members of such a group often feel a "calling" to the prayer ministry. They are spiritually advanced and experienced in prayer and small group intercession. They use methods they have studied previously and practiced successfully, such as visualizing, in their own ways, God's help going to the one prayed for—for example, peace coming to a troubled person, a sad person becoming joyful, a material need being fulfilled, a sick person being healed. (Many books on prayer teach this technique and in recent years some medical doctors have begun training their patients in healing visualization, with a percentage of success.)

This group often does not have a leader and, aside from perhaps a few procedural guidelines, its structure is spontaneous.

When it forms, the group agrees how much will be said about the problems of people for whom they pray. Some people feel a need to know what the problem is in order to pray specifically; others feel they would rather pray more generally and that knowledge of a serious illness, for instance, would subconsciously weaken their faith and block the flow of prayer energy. (Since the 1960s scientists in laboratory experiments have been measuring actual energy flow from people in prayer.)

Prayers in this group, whether silent or audible, are longer and more concentrated than in other groups. There is a lot more silence as members commune with God or silently continue a prayer that was said aloud.

Some prayer groups invite a person who is to be prayed for to join them for one or more sessions, so that they may pray in person for him. This is especially done in a group which practices the laying-on of hands as clergy do in healing services. If a person is too ill to go out, the group goes to his bedside. They all lay hands on the patient, and either have spontaneous audible prayer, or one person prays aloud and the rest silently. The patient also prays if he wishes.

One important rule to remember about praying for others: *do not discuss this outside the group*. The person who requests prayer does not want his need or problem or illness to be gossiped about. He entrusts you with a confidence when he asks you to pray for him and he has the right to expect you to keep it!

An intercession group should *not* be organized in the same

way as any other group. It is imperative that people meeting for intercessory prayer share the same basic beliefs about prayer and its efficacy, that they have a spiritual affinity for one another, that they feel mutual deep affection, and that they have no personality conflicts among themselves. If one such conflict does develop, those involved should seek immediate resolution and healing of feelings or leave the group until it comes about. The reason for this has to do with prayer principles relating to harmony in an intercession group.

This kind of group seems to "just happen." Usually, one who feels drawn to a prayer ministry will pray that God will put him in contact with others who feel such a desire, so that they may pray together. In time, this comes about in various ways. Members may bring new persons into the group from time to time, but they must be brought in under the same criteria. People should *never be sent* to such a group.

The most interesting way I have ever known God to call together a prayer group happened to Ed and me. As it turned out, this group was to serve two purposes—intercession and the sponsorship of a School of Pastoral Care in the Buffalo area! The threads of God's plan go back ten years previous when we were new in Buffalo and looking for an Episcopal church with a small group (a rare commodity in those days!). Through an unexpected contact with an Episcopal priest, Ed found a group meeting weekly in the home of Harlan and Lucy Klepfer, with whom we since have shared much ministry. We attended this group for two or three years, during which time a Methodist couple, Hugh and Libby Parker, joined the group.

Several years later, I needed someone to help me with housework, and I called the State employment office. The woman on the domestic desk had gone to lunch and Hugh Parker answered her phone (I didn't even know he worked there). During the conversation he asked if Ed and I would speak at his weekly current events discussion group at the nearby Presbyterian Home (residence for the elderly). We did this, each giving our biographical witness, and Ed returned twice to show his slides of Japan (his field is Asian history). They found him so interesting that they asked him to take morning chapel services periodically. Ed began going early for breakfast with the staff and met the Reverend Robert M. Armstrong, Director of the Presbyterian Homes of Western New York. In conversation, Ed asked if any prayer for healing was going on in this home. Bob referred him to the Administrator, Ruthie Hunt, R.N., who had just begun studying Agnes Sanford's books. Ruthie's response was tentative, so Ed dropped the subject.

Several months later, in May 1977, Ruthie called and asked if Ed would attend a meeting with her at the home of a friend, Esther Crane, to talk about one of Sanford's books. Also at the meeting were Bob Armstrong and his wife, Priscilla, and I. But we never did discuss the book! Instead, we each shared where we were spiritually and why we were interested in spiritual healing. Someone passed around a newsletter from the School of Pastoral Care. By the end of the evening, we all felt that God was leading us to sponsor a School in the Buffalo area, which we did in May 1978. Attending were physicians, nurses, clergy, counselors, and lay people with personal ministries. The response was so enthusiastic that the School became an annual event for four years.

During that year, we began meeting monthly for the purpose (we thought) of working out all the plans and details that go into sponsoring a five-day retreat for sixty-two people. But God had other plans! We did spend a few minutes each time discussing the School's progress, but the rest of the evening was always spent sharing what Christ was doing in our lives and in prayer for the School, the Presbyterian Homes, our individual churches and clergy, our lay ministries, and the problems and illnesses of ourselves, our families, and friends. In addition, Esther Crane began leading a study and prayer group for the residents of the nearby Home, and Ruthie Hunt began one for the staff.

After the School was over, no one doubted that we would

keep meeting for sharing and intercession. After the first School, we added several new members to the group, including two Catholic priests and a Catholic physician—a truly ecumenical gathering! We met for five years until our schedules changed.

I share this story with you as an example of God's infinite ways of bringing people together for His purposes.

It is not within the scope of this book to go further into depth on prayer and the intercession ministry. There are excellent books on these subjects by such spiritual leaders as Morton Kelsey, Francis MacNutt, Dennis and Matthew Linn, Agnes Sanford, Emily Gardiner Neal, Robert and Marjorie Hall, Donald Hultstrand, Helen Shoemaker, Andrew Murray, Evelyn Underhill, Thomas H. Green, Maxie Dunnam, Charles Whiston, and others.

Information on good study books is available from five organizations listed in the appendix: Anglican Fellowship of Prayer; Bible Reading Fellowship; Episcopal Center for Evangelism; International Order of St. Luke the Physician; and School of Pastoral Care.

# 6

# Element Three—Verbal Witnessing and Sharing of Insights

I N the sharing of insights, answered prayer, and the new things God is doing in the lives of group members (many of which relate to their study and prayer together), it becomes obvious that the witness is the common denominator in group life, the element which pervades and connects other elements. Such sharing comes about naturally within the context of the Christian small group as defined here.

Especially within an interdenominational group, the witness is invaluable for three reasons: (1) It provides a spiritual link among all the members. (2) It supplements their common belief in the Trinity. (3) The spiritual unity it creates prevents arguments from developing over theology, doctrine, and practice.

The witnessing element in a small group is very faith-strengthening (for reasons given in Part I, Chapter 2), but its effectiveness is multiplied in a group for the same reasons that the effectiveness of studying a book is multiplied in a group. Many different insights and experiences of God's current activity give continuing new evidence of the credibility of Christianity, enhancing intellectual acceptance and exchange.

For this reason, witnessing to searchers within a small group context is the most effective way to reach them. In only one meeting they hear perhaps dozens of stories of God's action in people's daily lives. The small group into which searchers are brought must have witnessing as its basic or only element because they are thinking, "I'm searching for something, but I'm not sure what it is," or "I'm searching for God," or "I believe in God, but I don't know if I believe in Christ," or "I'm looking for meaning in life," or "I want to find out who I am," or "I've got a problem I can't face or can't solve," or something similar. What they need is *evidence* that God is really there, that He is personal, that He loves them, that He accepts them as they are, that He can make them better, that He and they can communicate in prayer, that He acts in their lives. They want to know whether God can give their lives meaning, reveal their identity, provide guidance and strength, and fulfill their needs. The witness of others sharing such experiences is the most direct, efficient, and rapid method to show them where their answers are. (Part II, Chapter 17, "How To Organize A Small Group," discusses groups for searchers.)

To include the element of witness in your group, you may set aside a specific time in which members will share what God has been doing in their lives since the last meeting. Usually this is done first, since it sets the tone for study and prayer or other elements, but there is no rule, and it may be included at any point. The type of witnessing that comes about during book discussion is more of the insight type and of experiences that occurred in the past that are brought to mind by the material, although recent experiences will be included. Therefore, you will have witnessing throughout the discussion if the guidelines in Part II, Chapter 4 are followed. Whether or not you also set aside a time specifically for this element depends on how much emphasis your group wants on it.

As with prayer and book study, members may witness spontaneously or in turn. I prefer the spontaneous method because no member will have something to share at every meeting, and this allows one who does not to refrain from speaking without having to "pass" his turn. Witnessing is different from prayer and book discussion because you can compose a prayer and read the book in advance, but God's response to you or His initiation of an action in your life are experiences over which you have no control other than being receptive. Even if you have nothing to share for several meetings, that does not necessarily mean there is something wrong, so you should not feel that there is a problem if God has not done anything easily discernible in your life recently. The idea of group witnessing is *not* to try to have experiences to witness about but, on the contrary, to share what experiences do occur as you endeavor to live in God's grace day by day.

# 7

# Element Four—Meditation

MEDITATION means different things to different people. Usually, we think of this as something we do alone, if we ever have time! Belonging to a meditation group helps those who like to meditate keep the discipline of a time and place. I have found group and private meditation to be quite different, although both have their advantages and are beneficial. (We will cover only group meditation here.)

I see group meditation as having more of a communicative element than a learning or sharing one. We are communicating with God on a concentrated, conscious level and with others on a subconscious level. Jesus said that He is present where Christians are gathered together, so group meditation enriches our realization of our unity with God and each other.

Formats vary, depending on the leadership and on whether or not meditation is the sole element of the group.

If you have a person gifted at extemporaneous meditative recitation or with access to good meditation material, that person will probably lead the group each time. Otherwise, members may take turns selecting and reading material, or each member may bring one reading every time, but then there is the risk of listening to a lot of superfluous things unless the members are all spiritually advanced and in tune with one another's consciousness. Meditation groups, like true prayer groups, are best created by the conveners seeking those of their own spiritual level and temperament.

Some groups have more reading than silence, others more silence. Most alternate readings and silence, but the reading may be all at the beginning with the rest of the time spent in silence. At the close, intercessory prayers may be offered, but the basic purpose of the true meditation group is not intercession unless its members want a dual function. In this case, the two elements of meditation and prayer would be balanced, with the meditation done either first or alternately with intercession.

When done as one element among several, meditation may last from five to fifteen minutes, including a reading and silent time. This may be done at whatever point the members feel that it is most effective.

The most meaningful meditation group I have ever attended is the one I am in now. It is called a "healing service," and it's conducted by a Protestant minister, who is extremely gifted at meditation and who has infinite printed resources. Much of what she says is extemporaneous, some is read, and a few one-sentence prayers are read aloud together. There are brief silent periods throughout the hour. She uses material from devotional books of the positive, affirming, uplifting kind. She also prays in a general way for human needs: spiritual understanding, guidance, good health, material abundance, etc. We close by reading several short prayers, aloud, together. By the end of the hour, my whole being is filled with peace, and I am much more in tune with God than when we began. It *is* a "healing service"!

This group is open because of the type it is, but many meditation groups are closed once the members feel it has "jelled." As with a true prayer group, people should never be sent to a meditation group unless it is set up on an open basis.

Group meditation should not take the place of private meditation, and you will understand why if you are involved in group meditation. It becomes obvious that if we begin each day attaining the level of spiritual consciousness we reach in a good meditation group, we would meet the day's challenges quite differently; or if we ended the day in meditation, we would sleep much better!

# 8

# Element Five—Singing and Praising

THE type of small group which meets for extemporaneous song, praise, and other related activities is unfamiliar to most mainstream Christians. In fact, I personally do not care for it, but it is included here because it is a popular form among some Christians and is attractive to some young people. Such groups are usually called "prayer and praise meetings" and include prayer, singing, and witnessing, with some teaching, exhortation, and lots of Bible quoting. They are always open to anyone.

These groups do not have any particular format. Everyone just does his own thing as he feels the Holy Spirit leads him. However, I do not feel there is a sense of confusion since everyone listens to the one speaking or praying or reading, or joins in the song which one person begins. They all know by heart dozens of Christian songs: gospel, folk, and psalms set to music. Some songs are beautiful. Many others are either of the lively, hand-clapping variety or draggy and repetitive. The theology expressed in them is fundamentalist. Hymns are rarely sung except for the gospel type.

You hear a lot of people exclaiming softly, "Praise the Lord," "Bless you, Jesus," "Hallelujah," and "Amen," as things said strike home to them. Everything is spontaneous and uninhibited. People express needs for themselves and others, to which the response is immediate intercession. There are stories of answered prayer, for which prompt thanks is given. The teaching and exhorting may or may not be theologically sound. The scripture quoted or read is often chosen to support that which is being taught and to establish the validity of the exhortation.

There is much laughter and some tears, and a lot of joy and love is felt and expressed by hugging and kissing. Everyone leaves the meeting on a spiritual and emotional "high."

Young people especially like this type of group because of the freedom of expression, the informality, and the music—those who can play guitars bring them. If the youth of your church shun the organized activities you offer but attend "prayer and praise meetings," this is why.

I feel there are both desirable and undesirable aspects to such meetings. The free expression is helpful—some people are so tied up inside that it is a big help to be able to express themselves in such a relaxed atmsophere. But it is the kind of situation which encourages over-emotionalism in unstable people who often are drawn to any kind of meeting offering uncontrolled expression.

The witnessing and prayer are beneficial. Some of the teaching is good, if done by seasoned Christians who have studied with good teachers, but in this situation there are usually some self-styled Bible experts who think they understand everything in scripture and are eager to impart it. The same applies to the exhortations—sometimes they are on target, but too often the ones who exhort insist that you must have the same religious experiences they have had, in the same way, and they would be glad to give them to you!

These are some of the dangers I see in this type of group, but if this kind of activity appeals to you, seek out such a group and visit it. I do not recommend trying to form a "prayer and praise" group in your church unless your clergy favors it, and unless there are already at least a dozen of your own church members who have attended one and want to have their own. Invite the clergy to observe, if they do not want to participate, because most feel that this kind of group poses more of a threat to the stability and unity of the congregation than any other kind. If it does not pose a threat, the clergy may be a buffer between the group and the congregation if one is needed. If it does, then the clergy should know firsthand what the problems are and deal with them accordingly.

# 9

# Element Six—Introspective and Interpersonal Relating

S MALL groups for the purpose of introspective and interpersonal relating appeal to people who are drawn
to the psychological approach for a better understanding of
themselves and others, or who need some special methods—
such as role playing or mental games—to integrate them into the
group process. When Christian-related, this process is called by
some "relational theology." Through relational theology, a
group member learns to understand himself and others in the
context of relationships, person to person and person to God.
When not Christian-related, this process has various names and
is totally humanistic in its thrust.

The psychological approach is central to groups such as
Serendipity, Transactional Analysis, Sensitivity, Encounter,
Values Clarification and Awareness Development, among others. Relational theology is explicit in psychologically oriented
Christian groups. It is implicit in spiritually oriented Christian
groups where members learn the application of Christian theology
to their own lives and relationships as a built-in effect when the
group is coordinated properly.

Humanistic groups can be beneficial, as far as their approach goes, and have helped many when competent leaders were in charge. It is possible to receive psychological understanding in these groups. However, the focus can be way off and the conclusions isolated from, even in opposition to, spiritual principles, moral law, our relationship to God, and our place in a world created and pervaded by God as revealed in Christ. The leader of a purely humanistic group may be antagonistic to spiritual concepts and attempt to destroy the faith of the participants. For a person who is troubled or seeking to establish a relationship with God, such a situation can be devastating. Since our nature is essentially spiritual, the humanistic approach, whether antagonistic to Christianity or simply ignoring it, omits the main aspect necessary to a balanced understanding.

If your group members want to take the psychological approach, insist that the book they study or the program they follow be Christian-based, or at least Christian-related, so that they learn on all levels. *Balance* is the key, and the key to balance is the right leader. Seek out a well recommended Christian leader and have the whole group screen him before making the decision to hire him (these leaders charge because they do this professionally).

While other types of groups and elements do not need a leader with much training or experience, leaders for groups that do introspective and interpersonal relating *do*. There are four reasons:

1. There are specific techniques, some rather intricate, all fitting together in a certain progression to accomplish specific goals.

2. Instead of letting people arrive at various levels of understanding at their own pace, as is done in the other kinds of groups, all the members are led through definite steps, in the same way at the same time, to bring them all to a certain level together.

3. Depending on the psychological depth to which the group is led, the leader must know how to handle responses. In some

groups, not only are the members delving into their own psychological makeup, they are trying to help each other in this process.

4. The leader must be able to keep a balance in the group on the levels of concepts, goals, techniques, progression, and response.

By their nature, most such groups are closed after the first session.

It is not our purpose here to describe each of these groups. Books about them are available.

Personally speaking, this kind of group experience does nothing for me. I find it easy to integrate into group process, and I prefer to develop psychologically and emotionally at my own pace as an outgrowth of participation in a study, prayer, and witness group, and through structuring my life on the seven disciplines (see the next chapter).

# 10

## The Seven Disciplines as Feed and Fuel for a Lively Small Group

Alarge, attractive, red, black and white folding card, entitled "To Celebrate Life," and authored by the Reverend Claxton Monro, reads:

### DISCIPLINES FOR CHRISTIANS
#### To Celebrate Life in the Name of Jesus Christ Our Lord

Because of my awareness that God loves me, I will endeavor to:
1. Seek God's plan through a daily time of listening prayer and Bible reading.
2. Worship weekly in the Church with emphasis on Holy Communion.
3. Participate regularly in a weekly group for Christian sharing, study and prayer.
4. Give regularly a definite, grateful share of my income to the spread of God's kingdom through the Church and in the world.

And because I know that God loves my neighbor, I will endeavor to:
5. Pray daily for others with thanksgiving.

6. Exercise faithfully the particular ministries to which God calls me in the fellowship of the Church and in the world.
7. Speak and act so that my daily life is a witness to the love of God in Christ as I have come to know it.

## To Glorify God, To Strengthen the Church, To Help the World, To Grow in My Christian Life
### ALLELUIA!

No matter what type of small group you have, if you structure your spiritual life on the seven disciplines listed in the "Celebrate Life" card, two things will happen:

1. Your whole life will be upgraded spiritually and emotionally; it will be well balanced; you will mature in your relationship with God and others; and you will grow in understanding of yourself and your place in God's world. You will be fed spiritually and you will be exercising a ministry.

2. By sharing with one another the spiritual feeding and the events resulting from ministry, the members experience a very lively, meaningful, and sometimes downright exciting discussion! This sharing of the fruits of disciplines becomes fuel for the group, and members eagerly anticipate every meeting.

It has been my observation that groups which last long and give much to their members are those in which the members are faithfully keeping as many of these disciplines as possible, whether or not they are stated in exactly this format. The feeding and fueling action of these disciplines is a dynamic in small groups. When a group that seemed to have great potential fails, find out how well they kept these disciplines.

# 11

# The Personal Bond among Small Group Members

**O**NE of the greatest dividends of belonging to a Christian small group is the close personal bond that develops among all its members. Naturally, on a friendship level, you will be closer to some than others. But there is a relationship that transcends that natural affection which is based on human chemistry. I call it spiritual love; the Greeks call it *agape*. Whatever you call it, it is there, and it is tangibly felt.

When you belong to a small group whose members are learning together, praying together, sharing their lives and experiences, you soon get to know the other members as well as, if not better than, lifelong friends. Status, possessions, background, and other human common denominators cease to matter as a strong bond develops among them. Even if the group eventually disbands, that love and friendship is always felt. Of course, this bond is often the glue that holds together groups that are long-lived.

This is a dynamic that is difficult to explain and must be experienced to be understood.

# 12

# Length of Group Life

GROUPS come and groups go. I have known some that have lasted for years. I have known some that have broken up in a few months. The reasons groups break up are tangible and intangible. They usually concern such things as: studying material that is wrong for the group because it is too elementary or too advanced or not of real interest; getting bogged down in one type of material for too long; failure to study the assignment in advance; not keeping the daily prayer covenant, if there is one; failure to structure one's personal life on basic spiritual principles; failure to keep personal and group disciplines agreed to; lack of openness among group members; intellectualizing and impersonalizing the discussion; refusal of some members to participate in any important element; not following proper procedural guidelines; gossiping about group matters outside the meetings; and personality conflicts, especially if there is a person who is emotionally unstable (see Part II, Chapter 16, "Handling Problem People and Situations").

Another reason a group breaks up—which is not a bad one—is that some members attain greater spiritual maturity faster than others, and the only way to continue servicing everyone is to break up the group and re-form according to current interests. This must be done very tactfully, however, in order not to hurt or alienate the slower members.

Another good reason a group breaks up is that it has grown too large, because it is such a successful group that it has continually attracted new people. When a group reaches twelve to fifteen members, it should either limit its membership or break into two groups. This can be a difficult situation because members may have grown so close that they do not want to split up. The leader should take the initiative here. The deciding factor is whether the group is still functioning as it should with a large number. If not, and if members cannot determine any other way to split into two groups, they may simply flip a coin or draw numbered slips of paper.

If a group is faltering, it may be possible to correct the problem and enable it to return to a viable situation. But there are times when the group's life *should* be ended. When it has served its purpose it should be disbanded with thanksgiving. So many people mourn over the demise of a group because they think it should have gone on forever when that was not the case at all. Try to learn from mistakes and avoid them in your next group. But when a group is finished, "loose it and let it go."

Depending on the purposes of a group, its life may be open-ended or limited. Some groups form, planning to study one book or experience one closely interdependent series of sessions, and disband when completed. The advantage of this is that it is easier for some people to keep a short-term commitment faithfully than one that is long or open-ended. Many people are not willing to make an open-ended commitment, especially if they have had no previous group experience. Frequently, members of a limited group will develop such a close bond and get so much out of their sessions that they will choose to stay together for another period of time.

# 13

# Open and Closed Groups

SOME groups close membership during the study of a book or participation in a structured series, and let new people in at the beginning of the next one. Some let people come in at any time. Which is best depends on the type of book or experience.

If the series is one in which each chapter or cassette or session builds on the one before, or if the group is involved in specific short-term goals or progressive techniques, as in introspective and interpersonal relating, the group should be closed after beginning.

If the book is a simple one in which each chapter can stand alone, or the cassettes are not interdependent, and the group is not involved in anything requiring continuity for effectiveness, then there is no reason not to accept new members at any time. The group will frequently benefit thereby. Each group should decide its policy when it forms.

Some groups become so close that they feel a special bond and do not desire new members. Such groups have been accused of being ingrown. However, this is not necessarily exclusiveness but the sensing of spiritual harmony in receiving new insights, in ministering to one another, and in intercessory prayer. When this situation occurs, the group is truly experiencing its reason for being, and can be a great blessing for both its members and those for whom it prays. But this situation cannot be planned or created; it is one that evolves out of the right combination of membership and elements. You can be sure that when such a group does evolve, God's guidance was sought and followed, from its formation on through its every meeting. This is the kind of group which will last indefinitely.

As pointed out earlier, if the basic purpose of a group is prayer or the study of prayer, it will do better if the group is closed once it has "jelled." The reasons for this are mostly intangible but, experience has shown, nonetheless valid. They have to do with personal and spiritual harmony among members, as well as growth in the understanding and practice of the spiritual principles governing prayer.

When the basic function of a group is witnessing, then by its nature it is open because its purpose is to attract searchers and strengthen the faith of new Christians (see Part II, Chapter 17, "How To Organize A Small Group").

As previously stated, meditation groups may be set up on an open or closed basis, and groups for singing and praising are always open.

# 14

# Arrangements

### Frequency of Meetings

Weekly is best. There is real continuity to a group that meets weekly. Every member is truly committed to the group and its purposes. There is some sacrifice entailed in keeping a weekly commitment. The member must put the group first in a conflict of interests, except in unusual circumstances. However, if the group is accomplishing its purposes well, the members will not think of frequency as a sacrifice, but as a blessing.

A group can meet bi-weekly or monthly and still be a good experience, but with certain exceptions it will not be as meaningful in the total context of one's life. However, meeting bi-weekly or monthly is better than not at all.

### Time of Meetings

Set the time which is most convenient for the group members. Men's groups do best early in the morning before going to work, but they can also be successful at noontime, meeting at business places or private rooms in clubs or restaurants, in the downtown area. Businesswomen's groups usually do best in the evening, although some prefer the early morning, also.

Groups for wives and mothers who don't work outside the home are best held in the daytime—usually mid-morning. Couples' groups or mixed groups are best held on a weekday evening or a Sunday evening. Groups for youth are best held either after school or on a Sunday, either in the morning at the regular church school hour or in the evening. Groups for adults can also be successful during the church school hour, but then they do not fulfill the need for that mid-week spiritual lift that most group participants want.

### Length of Meetings

Set a closing time as well as an opening time and stick to them. Group members should be able to discipline themselves to arrive on time, and they should be able to count on leaving at a certain time—they may have baby sitters, they may have another commitment, or they may be just plain tired and want to get to bed. If the discussion is so lively that members want to carry it on longer, an opportunity should be given for those who must leave at the appointed time to do so.

Depending on the elements of the particular group and the ways in which they are carried out, one to two hours should be adequate for a group session. Make an estimate when you start a new group and then make adjustments later on, if warranted.

### Place of Meetings

I know a clergyman who says that in his parish women's groups fail at the church and succeed in the home. He says, "You can take a woman group leader and put her in the parish house with a group and she'll fail, and take the same woman and put her in a home with a group and she'll succeed. I don't understand why, but that's the way it works!" Nevertheless, there have been a few good women's groups meeting on and off at this church, but the women's groups meeting in homes have flourished. Conversely, men's groups have done well at the church.

Place depends on several factors, but there are no rigid rules about it. Groups that meet in the early morning are mostly men's groups, and they usually find the church a more convenient place for obvious reasons. It is often more centrally located than a member's home. There is not the problem of the early morning commotion, as families get ready for the day's work or school. A parish house is a very quiet, peaceful place at 6:00 or 7:00 A.M.! However, if the family is geared to it, if the physical set-up is conducive, and if the location is convenient to all members, the early morning group can meet successfully in a home.

A group that meets mid-morning is almost always composed of women. They usually prefer to meet in a home, whether the group is open or closed, especially if they are young wives and mothers living in a suburb. Newcomers are either brought in by a member or recommended by the clergy. I know of several groups of middle-aged and older women living in the city who meet at their churches, and this works out well for them.

If the group meets in the evening, it is usually a singles', a couples', or a businesswomen's group. If most of the members prefer meeting in a room at church, they should try it. If the group is open to everyone, meeting there is a convenience for newcomers. Most evening groups, however, prefer meeting in homes, whether the group is open or closed.

Youth groups should meet at the church because it is a "rallying point" and youth "drop in" and "drop out" randomly except for a committed core. Youth meeting in homes could run into various family problems, but it usually works out well if they meet at the rectory or in the youth leader's home, if the meeting place is well publicized.

There are different ways to choose homes for meetings. Some groups meet every time in one home, some change homes every meeting or monthly. There are advantages and disadvantages in both cases. It is simpler to meet in one home (I prefer it), but changing homes eases the duties of hosting it and the burden of driving long distances every time for some members. Each group must decide for itself.

Wherever the group meets, the room should be at a comfortable temperature, with comfortable chairs and good ventilation and adequate lighting (not too bright, but light enough to read without trouble). People should feel relaxed, so that their minds are not distracted by physical problems. Arrange the chairs more or less in a circle and comfortably close together. In this way, people can hear without straining. Never use a table: it gives a sense of barrier.

### Refreshments

This must also be decided by each group, but in any case, do not have anything elaborate. Refreshments are not really necessary at all because this is not a social occasion. However, some groups like to have light beverages and perhaps cookies or cake. If you do serve something, keep it simple, take turns purchasing it, and if it gets to be a burden, have the courage to say so and dispense with it.

Alcoholic beverages are a ''no no'' because the group is serious business and we want clear heads!

# 15

# Leadership Responsibilities

LEADERSHIP of a small group usually rotates among its members, unless you have a person who is an outstanding leader with spiritual maturity and group experience. Even so, such a leader should follow the same guidelines as the rotating leaders. Leadership rotates weekly, monthly, or with a change in study material.

If you are the leader of a small group, the major areas of your responsibility will be these: You will guide the discussion, try to keep it from becoming too abstract and impersonal, and keep it on the subject. You should also know when to let it stay off the subject temporarily for the benefit of one member or the whole group, and how to balance group goals and individual need if an emergency arises (for example, a person who shares a sorrow or a problem—sometimes the real purpose of that meeting is to minister to him). The direction of leadership at those times will depend on common sense, understanding of group goals, and sensitivity to members' needs. In such cases, pray silently for God's guidance. You must be flexible, for rigidity can stifle the Holy Spirit's work, but you must not be so flexible that there is little format or continuity.

It is desirable that every member should feel open to the others and participate in all elements. Your attitude as leader can make the difference. You should gently encourage members who are reluctant to participate to feel at ease and to enter into the element of which they feel shy. The way this is done and the frequency of it will vary. It should be done in a sensitive, loving, and nonjudgmental manner. Sometimes a person's lack of participation is best left alone, allowing him to grow to that point slowly.

In preparation for the meeting, read the assignment ahead of time. Make notes about significant points, including why they were meaningful to you and any personal experience that relates to them. Actually, everyone should do this. The more thought that participants have given to the assigned reading, the deeper and more lively will be the discussion. You might prepare questions that will stimulate personal sharing.

The leader should be prepared to pray at the beginning and end of the meeting, and whenever a need for prayer arises. Others may give opening and closing prayers and pray for particular needs, but the leader must be prepared to do it himself. If you are leading and if you are not adept at praying spontaneously, then you may write opening and closing prayers beforehand and read them. (I did this the first few times.) But the style should be informal and you must soon wean yourself away from written prayers. There is nothing wrong in using one or two prayers from books, but one of the advantages of small group participation is learning to pray aloud informally, and when everyone feels at ease doing it the experience is beautiful.

If the group wants to keep a prayer list, determine specific guidelines and see that members observe them. Check, from time to time, whether or not they are keeping the covenant fairly consistently and want to continue. Encourage honest response and drop it if they are not enthusiastic. Set up a prayer chain if they want one. (Refer to Part II, Chapter 5.)

Whatever group disciplines and procedures are agreed to—and these should be discussed and understood in the first meeting—become the leader's responsibility to carry out. There usually will be no problems about them if you keep them in mind and are consistent in their implementation.

Stress the importance of keeping any personal disciplines agreed to, such as the seven disciplines (Part II, Chapter 10), and stimulate sharing about this in the group.

It is assumed that since the group members are Christians, their lives are based on certain spiritual principles expressed in the Bible. A Christian who is out of tune with this lifestyle will either eventually drop out of the group or will be helped to spiritual maturity by it. The leader's responsibility to such a person is to create an atmosphere of love and *personal* acceptance, while upholding basic spiritual principles by example and through group discussion. You do not have to approve of the sin to love the sinner!

Sometimes people will share experiences or feelings in their group which they would never mention elsewhere. When this happens, it indicates that there is trust among them, and this is one of the most important aspects of a good group relationship. As leader, remind them, when necessary, that what is said in the group should not be repeated outside. This is not a common problem, but one that should be handled if it arises, even to the extent of asking a constant offender to leave the group. A group's purposes will not be served, and it will soon break up, if members feel they must watch what they say.

The group leader has the responsibility for handling any problem persons and situations, although this responsibility is shared by all group members. (See the next chapter.)

For each group there must be a person responsible for resources: books, cassettes, study plans, etc. It may be the leader or the clergy or a knowledgeable contact person, but it is vital to match the proper study material with the area of interest and spiritual level of the group. You will encounter problems if you give a book to a group which is very far off the general spiritual level of its members, even if it is on a subject of their interest. This is especially true in the areas of prayer, spiritual healing, spiritual gifts, and the like. As you read extensively in these fields and others, you will acquire a knowledge of what is beginning, intermediate, and advanced. But this takes time, so seek out someone who is already well read on the various Christian subjects which are studied in small groups, if you do not feel able to make this determination.

Choose books written in such a way that the reader can identify the subject matter with his own personal life and experience. Thus, he can share in the group how he sees this as applicable to himself, his faith, his prayer life, his worship, his spiritual disciplines, his ministries, etc. This is not to say that it cannot be an intellectual book—it can. Many books, such as some by C. S. Lewis and Morton Kelsey, lend themselves to this kind of discussion. But again, it must be on the spiritual level corresponding to that of the group.

The question arises here: how do you discern the spiritual level of the group? This is an intangible thing and it need not be judgmental. What are the books they have read? Have they ever been in a small group before? What kind? What elements? For how long? How did they respond? What is their current area of major interest? What study and experience have they had in this area? The answers to these questions should tell you a lot. If you are still in doubt, it is always safe to start with the New Testament, common ground for every Christian on any level.

In recent years, beginning groups have had impressive success with the book-cassette series, *The Edge Of Adventure*,* and its sequel, *Living The Adventure*.** Two old classics, that have been staples of new small groups for years, are *The Will Of God*† and *The Christian's Secret Of A Happy Life*.‡ For a small group launching vehicle that can be used as a week-

---

* Keith Miller and Bruce Larson, *The Edge Of Aventure,* Word Books, Waco, Texas, 1974.

** Keith Miller and Bruce Larson, *Living The Adventure,* Word Books, Waco, Texas, 1975.

† Leslie D. Weatherhead, *The Will of God,* Abingdon Press, Nashville, Tennessee, 1944, 1972.

‡ Hannah Whitall Smith, *The Christian's Secret Of A Happy Life,* Fleming H. Revell Company, Old Tappan, New Jersey, 1952, 1970.

end retreat or as a 5-week series, the Aurora Conference Centre's *Experiencing Christian Community*\* is excellent.

There is another area of intermittent leadership responsibility. Since the kind of small group we are discussing is a Christian community in addition to whatever else it may be, members will desire to help one another in crisis. The leader should be certain that all members are made aware of emergencies for prayer and action as they feel led.

\* Graham H. Tucker and Douglas C. Blackwell, *Experiencing Christian Community, A Programme Manual For Christian Community Development In The Local Congregation,* Aurora Conference Centre, Aurora, Ontario L4G 3G8.

# 16

# Handling Problem People and Situations

WHENEVER we interact with others, especially in the small group context, we occasionally will encounter problem people, some who can be absorbed by the group if they are controlled, and some who create unacceptable situations because they cannot be controlled. These are guidelines for handling the most prevalent problems arising in small groups.

Prevention is better than cure, so do not accept or place in a group someone who is mentally ill or has deep emotional problems. This is the fastest way to destroy a group, and it does not help the problem person one bit. Such a person simply is not capable of following group guidelines and disciplines, and everyone will be constantly dealing with him instead of doing what they are gathered to do—and that is why the group will not function for long.

If you feel that such a person needs the benefits of belonging to a small group, seek the help of your clergy or a social worker who can refer him to a specialized group for people with his particular problem (that is, professionally led therapy groups, Recovery, Alcoholics Anonymous, drug rehabilitation groups, etc.). A small group cannot be all things to all people, and even if group members want to help a troubled person, amateur counseling will fail and may do more harm than good.

If a person manifests such problems *after* joining a group, a tactful way must be found to get him out of the group. The best way I know is to have a leader of the type of group he should be in invite him to that group. If he does attend, he may become so involved in it and find his needs so much better met that he may leave your group voluntarily. Another solution is to disband the group at the end of the particular book or book of the Bible being studied. Then re-form the next month, meeting at another place, without the problem person.

Another method is simply to talk to him privately in a loving but firm manner, explaining that everyone in the group must keep the guidelines and disciplines, and that if he cannot comply, you must ask him to leave the group, although you hope this won't be necessary. He may improve and become tolerable, and even receive help from his association with the group, if his instability is not too acute. If not, he may leave, blaming group members. Creating an intolerable situation and then feeling wronged when others try to deal with it is a classic symptom of emotional illness. If you speak with him compassionately, there is no reason to feel guilty if a negative reaction results. Each such person and the problems he creates are different. The group leader and members need to consider, prayerfully, their response. The clergy may be of help in handling such problems.

Sometimes there will be a person in a group who gives long and detailed recitals of troubles, illnesses, deaths, personality conflicts, and the like. This person may not be emotionally ill, but simply overwhelmed and burdened by many great problems. Again, such a person must be controlled, because if this goes to the extreme, the group may not be destroyed, but it certainly will be weakened and some members will drop out.

One way to handle this is to break in with a comment such as, "That really is a bad situation (or big problem) and we don't know the answer, but God does, so why don't we say a prayer about it right now." This is where extemporaneous prayer comes in handy, but it must be a sincere prayer, not just a gimmick to quiet someone. God does answer prayer, and when this person begins to recognize that God is helping him, his attitude may improve vastly, and his life can even change. Sometimes such people join a small group only to gain a sympathetic ear, and if they are handled rightly, they begin to seek God's help in prayer and to try to help themselves, which they may not have done before.

However, these people take a lot of patience when they go to the extreme. Some will not be stopped by prayers, some do not want to help themselves. In such a case, you must have a private talk with him, as you did with the other kind of problem person, explaining that the group is not equipped to give advice, and that its time is limited and must be spent on the purpose for which it is gathered. Suggest he seek counsel from the clergy or some qualified person or agency, and make the connection for him if he is willing. Urge him to keep the disciplines and stay within the guidelines of the group. Pray with him and pray for him in your daily prayer time. If handled firmly, this person will finally leave the group if all he wanted was sympathy, or stay and become a normally participating member if he really wanted help.

Another type of problem person who attends groups is one who dominates the discussion. This may be the result of over-enthusiasm, perhaps due to the newness of his Christian life. It could be that his life situation is such that no one listens to him except his group. Or perhaps the person is simply a know-it-all who has an opinion about everything, who argues, criticizes, or complains. This type will destroy a group in short order. When he is talking, break in and say, "We are getting a little off the track," or "I sympathize, but we are really not here to deal with that subject," or "I appreciate your feelings, but you have shared several things and I would like to hear from those who have not had an opportunity to say very much.'' Then ask someone else a pertinent question to get the discussion back in gear. If the problem person is not too dense, he may realize he is dominating and quiet down. He may gradually improve as he continues meeting with the group and gets the idea that the discussion is share and share alike! If he does not, you may either have to disband and re-form without him or speak to him privately, being quite candid about his domination and cross-purposes with the group, clearly explaining again the guidelines and disciplines. Then ask him to cooperate or leave the group. With this type, you must be quite blunt, but you can do it in a kind way!

One kind of problem situation that can arise in groups with mothers of young children is that the mother brings her baby or small child to the meeting or, if it is held in her home, allows the children to interrupt constantly. This can be most distracting and time-wasting. A group needs quiet surroundings for concentration and it cannot take too much interruption and still function effectively. Therefore, sitters should be arranged for, either at the church or at a member's home where the group is not meeting.

Another problem situation may develop even if the group has no problem people. Sometimes, even though the guidelines and disciplines are being followed well, the group may seem dull or shallow. Naturally, the quality of meetings will vary because, no matter how interesting a group is, few will have fascinating, in-depth discussions every time. Also, each member's reaction and response will vary. But if more meetings are boring than interesting, something should be done. First, find out if everyone feels the same way about it. This may be done privately or by asking the group. Pray silently for honest responses! If they agree, then have the group discuss what to do about it.

Do you need a change in study material? Are the members able to relate it to personal Christian living? Is everyone entering fully into the discussion and other elements? Is everyone trying to keep basic personal spiritual disciplines? Are they sharing results with the group? Are there any serious personality conflicts within the group? Leader and members should share in defining problems and seeking solutions.

If problems cannot be pinpointed or remedies fail, then the group has outlived its usefulness and should be disbanded with thanksgiving. One meaningful way to do this is to have a celebration of Holy Communion at the last meeting.

# 17

# How to Organize a Small Group

THE most frequently asked question regarding a small group is, "How do you get it started?" Unfortunately, there are no pat answers. If you ask a dozen people how their groups were organized, you will get a dozen different answers! But there are some helpful guidelines.

This chapter title refers to "a" small group because it is better to start with one and build from there, unless many people in your church are requesting groups. I know of nothing else that will create such interest in and openness to small groups as a renewal event held *within* the parish, such as those sponsored by Faith Alive, Lay Witness Mission, Festival of Faith, Anglican Fellowship of Prayer, Order of St. Luke, and others. Although a small group may be an offshoot of events held *outside* the parish, such as Faith/At/Work, Cursillo, and Marriage Encounter, they usually do not create a demand for groups within the parish, because participants of each event are from many churches. Periodic parish renewal events are also excellent catalysts for congregational renewal, recommitment, lay ministry, and for enlivening existing groups. (See Appendix for addresses of renewal organizations.)

Most small groups will be for committed Christians, even groups formed as a result of a renewal event, because such

132

events are for the purpose of deepening and enlivening the faith the congregation already has, not for evangelism. However, a renewal event may become an evangelistic event for those church members who have never previously made a Christian commitment and for those outsiders who are invited. In forming a small group for Christians, it is best to gear it to a beginning level if the people to be in it have never had a group experience. If they stay together long enough, they will grow spiritually and most will want to go into greater depth. The ones who do will either add new elements or break off into a new group.

If you have several people interested in a group, ask them what they need or desire. Do they want to know more about the Bible? To learn to pray more effectively? To grow in faith and grace? To learn how to apply their faith to daily life and problems? To study any particular subject, such as spiritual healing? To know themselves better? Do they have any special circumstances of life in common with which they need help and encouragement?

If you want to start a group but do not know who else would be interested, determine for yourself what purposes you would like the group to fulfill. What are your own needs? What do you want to know more about? Pray that God will show you or send to you those who would be right for the group. This is a prayer you can expect to be answered because groups have been created this way many times. However, the answer may surprise you as people join the group whom you would not have thought would be interested or would "fit in."

One of my first groups was composed of several young women like myself, in our twenties and early thirties. We met weekly, shared the same interests and spiritual needs, and were drawn personally closer with each meeting. Then the rector sent into the group Mrs. Clara Knotts, a lady in her eighties! Outwardly we made her welcome, but inwardly we felt she would put a damper on the group. From the first meeting, she made herself the most beloved of all, with the love, joy, wit, and wisdom she shared with us from her almost century-long walk with Christ.

Whether you know people who want a group or you are trying to start one alone, talk with your minister, asking his ideas and support. In what ways would he like to see his people grow spiritually? He knows the needs of a wide spectrum of his congregation and can help you determine which needs might be met through small group experience. There are many ways in which he can support and promote groups. (See the next chapter.)

To begin a new group, you must first consider for whom you are creating it, their needs and interests, and what purposes should be served. Then choose the elements and format. As noted previously, Christians and searchers usually cannot be serviced in the same group because their spiritual needs are too divergent. Faith in a triune God is assumed by members of groups for Christians, and is the basis for all they do. Therefore, no time is wasted debating basic Christian theology, although personal interpretation may enter into the discussions as members seek deeper insights. Searchers do not know what they believe and are seeking evidence to guide them. They need an evangelistic group.

The difference between groups for Christians and groups for searchers is like the difference between nurturing fish in a home tank and trying to capture fish in a lake. Both groups are hungry, but one lives in close community and knows where its food comes from, and the other is scattered and must be lured to the food source. The ones in the tank know what they are getting and expect it regularly. The ones in the lake do not. You may give both groups the same food, but you must go about it in different ways!

Witnessing should be the only or main function of the evangelistic group. If you have teaching, Scripture reading or singing, go lightly and choose selections that are short and easy to comprehend. All but the most basic and simple teaching should be left to classes to which you should refer searchers who express interest in learning more. A person who is not sure what he believes may attend classes at the same time as he attends an evangelistic group, and some classes can become part of the evangelistic process. The unsure ones generally will not start out that way because the purposes of classes are to clarify the faith one already has; to provide a deeper understanding of scripture, theology, and doctrine; to explain the nature of the church today and as it has developed through the ages—all subjects infinitely more vital to a person who has already made a commitment to Jesus Christ.

An evangelistic group must have a constant influx of different Christians visiting and witnessing for it to fulfill its purpose. Before you start this kind of group, be sure you have enough people who can witness to cover every meeting for at least a year. By that time, you will be adding others who have been brought along in the group, and the original speakers will have new experiences to relate. Schedule the speakers ahead of time. If you have more than one speaker at a meeting, try to mix them—men and women, young and old, professionals and laborers, Catholic, Anglican, and Protestant. These should be lay persons with rare exceptions. Lay persons are more believable to searchers. Most clergy tend to preach or teach instead of witness. I have heard countless searchers say that they were not impressed by clergy they had heard because "they are paid to say those things."

Choose speakers on whom you can rely to follow the witnessing guidelines in Part I, Chapter 5. It is the responsibility of the leader to communicate these guidelines to speakers.

There must be a core group of a few people who organize and lead the meeting each time. These people must have a commitment to evangelism since this type of group is more a ministry than a spiritual growth vehicle, although it is always helpful to hear a witness. Others are needed to attend the group, to undergird it with prayer, to offer friendship to newcomers, and often to listen to their problems and pray with them. After the first two meetings of the evangelistic group in my Buffalo church, visitors asked me to pray with them about problems they were facing in the coming week.

The clergy may be present, depending on how the group is set up and what other, if any, activities accompany the meeting. (See the next chapter.)

Evangelistic groups may be held at the church or in homes, and formats vary widely, sometimes changing with time. I have experienced four types of such groups, two in churches and two in homes.

For five years at my Buffalo church we had a group the first Sunday of each month, meeting in a small dining room in the parish hall. We began with a light supper from 6:00 to 7:00 P.M., for which there was no charge, although we did accept up to $1.00 as a donation. From 7:00 to 8:00 P.M., three people gave their biographical witnesses for up to twenty minutes each (we were strict on the time limit). At 8:00 P.M. we had five to ten minutes of informal prayers led by the rector, either in the dining room or in the adjacent chapel. We had an intercessory prayer box at the door and invited anyone to put in prayer requests or thanksgivings to be offered to God during the week by the church's intercession group.

At my former parish in Houston we had a weekly Sunday evening prayer service with hymns, led by the rector in the church. Two persons, usually a man and a woman, witnessed for about fifteen minutes each, one giving a biographical witness and one witnessing on how one of the seven disciplines (Part II, Chapter 10) was making a difference in his life. After the service we went into the parish house for an hour, breaking into men's and women's groups. In this way, husbands and wives felt more free to participate in the discussion, and they were in groups with those sharing similar interests. The only element in those groups was witnessing. Each group had one or two leaders who started the discussion by sharing what was meaningful to them in the church witnesses, or something that had happened in their own lives recently, or how one of the seven disciplines was helping them. Afterwards, there was a social hour with coffee, cookies, and a book table.

In Part II, Chapter 3, I mentioned the two home evangelistic groups in which I have participated, called "house churches." Many searchers came to a faith in Christ there before they ever got to church! One met at 8:00 P.M. every Thursday night, changing homes monthly. A burning torch was placed in the front yard for both aesthetic and practical reasons: to symbolize the Holy Spirit and to help visitors find the house. A man and woman each gave a biographical witness, with no time limit. Between speakers and after the second speaker, light refreshments were served and discussion ensued. There were no other elements. The clergyman usually did not attend the home meetings.

The other home group met every Friday at 8:00 P.M., and always in the same house. One or two speakers witnessed, and discussion followed. There was singing, Scripture reading, and prayer, followed by a social time with light refreshments. This particular meeting originally began as a bridge from Alcoholics Anonymous to the church and, through the Friday meetings combined with counseling during the week, an in-depth ministry developed to alcoholics, drug addicts, prostitutes, prisoners, and other troubled people. Gradually it drew people from all backgrounds and became a source of inspiration to Christians as well as searchers.

To create a small group in the marketplace—at your place of work or in a downtown location—it is helpful to have the counsel of those experienced in this aspect. Here again, there are as many ways to organize as there are organizers! I consider the expert in this field to be an interdenominational organization called "The Pittsburgh Experiment."* which has been working in this field since 1955. Its ministry is the formation of

---

*The Pittsburgh Experiment, 1802 Investment Building, Pittsburgh, Pa. 15222.

small groups in businesses and factories, for the purpose of spiritual nourishment and evangelism to both management and labor.

Because of their setting in the market place, these groups are less highly structured than groups in churches and homes, and they service both searchers and Christians on a basic level. The groups meet weekly. They are open and usually have a core who attend regularly and some who visit. In all groups the elements are faith sharing and prayer. Retreats and programs in personal prayer and study are also offered. In 1962, Employment Anonymous groups were added to give encouragement and spiritual sustenance to unemployed men and women.

The Pittsburgh Experiment is a full-time ministry whose directors have varied in denomination over the years. This is another ministry begun by the late Reverend Samuel M. Shoemaker. Recently, due to requests from many other cities for help in starting a similar ministry, The Pittsburgh Experiment and Guideposts formed The Guideposts National Experiment.

A younger but just as vibrant a marketplace ministry is the King-Bay Chaplaincy,* begun in 1978 in downtown Toronto. In addition to small groups for prayer, faith sharing and Bible study, King-Bay offers public forums, worship services, and seminars on stress, career evaluation and planning, values and ethics, the Christian world view in a business culture office politics and pressures, the future urban church, and other subjects. For companies, King-Bay's Management Support System provides development and implementation of a value-based management program. For those who want to deepen their faith, know themselves better, and find God's plan for their lives, King-Bay conducts a "Discovery Weekend" retreat.

---

*King-Bay Chaplaincy, Box 175, Toronto Dominion Centre, Toronto, Ontario M5K 1H6.

# 18

# The Backing of the Parish Clergy

THE parish clergy do not have to back the concept of small groups for one to be *formed,* but the clergy do have to back it to the hilt in order for small groups to *flourish.* Small groups must be integrated into the total parish structure in order to have a meaningful impact on the life of the congregation.

If your priest or minister opposes the concept of small groups, discuss it with him. Bringing the reluctant minister into the process may create a new openness toward the idea. By seeking his counsel, you are minimizing the seeming threat; you are submitting to his authority; you are showing respect for him and his position. Even if he does not cooperate, he knows that the communication lines are open.

You can always get together a group to meet in your home which has nothing to do with the church officially. Under those circumstances, if you find enough people for one group you will be doing well since you cannot promote it through any of the usual means of parish information dissemination. You also have to consider the fact that if you have official status in the church, such as teacher, lay minister, or member of the governing body, promoting something privately to which the clergy is opposed could be counterproductive, especially if the opposition is vehement. Seek God's guidance about this. You can always attend a group elsewhere.

I once heard a minister say, "Prayer groups are dangerous!" (He was using the term "prayer group" to include all small groups.) Some clergy fear that things could get out of hand in a group where everyone is a learner and no one a teacher; or that something contrary to the church's theology or doctrine could be said and accepted since he is not there to correct it; or that some scripture could be interpreted incorrectly; or that counseling on a shallow level could be given to someone with deep emotional problems, making him worse; or that some fanatic could take control of the group, creating other fanatics and therefore producing problems spilling over into parish life. Such problems have occurred, but the reason is that those groups were formed by people unqualified to lead them, and there was no liaison with the clergy or any mature, experienced group coordinator, and therefore no training or guidelines.

An inexperienced leader can conduct a good group, given the right motives, guidelines, and participants, but if there is a problem with one of these areas, trouble often lies ahead. So if lay people want to form a group and the minister is opposed, he could be creating the very problems he feared!

The clergy must understand the value of small groups in the evangelism process for evangelism groups to be formed. I know of no way to have such groups without their complete and enthusiastic cooperation, since these groups must be part of an over-all parish evangelism program if they are to have any appreciable impact, and they need facilities and financing.

Many clergy, although not opposed, do not see the value in small group experience. At least, these clergy will often let you use the normal communication channels to the parish membership, and some will include it in their Sunday announcements. But again, even if the clergy do all this and do not back it enthusiastically in other ways, you may have one or two groups meeting, but they will not flourish and you will not get much "new blood."

If the minister does understand the value of small groups and he is enthusiastic, then there are several ways he can help you to organize and promote them. (I say "he" can help "you" because this is basically a lay activity. It is something you do with his guidance more than something he does with your help!)

1. He can preach about the value of small group experience in the context of parish life, including a description of the types of groups he would like to have.

2. He can write articles in the church newsletter encouraging people to participate. He should include days, times, places, and purposes of specific groups as they are formed.

3. He can include the groups in the list of activities in the Sunday bulletin. He can mention them in announcements.

4. He can designate a parish coordinator or lay minister for small groups to be the contact person, the resource person, the one who creates new groups, helps select elements and study material, and refers new members.

5. One of the most important things he can do is to refer to small groups people whom he counsels. One clergyman I know refuses long-term counseling cases unless, during the counseling period, the person will attend a weekly small group meeting for study, prayer, and witnessing. He is a gifted counselor but claims that his sessions are twice as effective and half as prolonged if the person is also in a small group.

6. He can visit the groups periodically, perhaps bringing Communion. This creates a closer liaison between him and the groups and gives them opportunity to discuss any problems. If he participates regularly in a group, he should have the same role as everyone else and should not be expected always to lead or to interpret everything so that he assumes the role of teacher. Although in my experience the clergy did not attend the home evangelism meetings, there is no reason why they should not. More often, they attend those at church. I feel that the minister

should attend these church meetings because his presence says that this is an official and integral part of the church's ministry.

7. He can schedule periodic parish renewal events, giving full backing to them and timely guidance to follow-up activities. Such activities enrich groups and vice versa.

Additional methods should be used to promote small groups whose sole or primary purpose is evangelism. The clergy should promote these groups within the parish in the same way as other groups. For promotion outside, clergy and parishioners must work as a team. Personal invitations are probably the most effective method of bringing searchers to home evangelism groups. Times and addresses of these groups should be published weekly and be available by phone from the church office. For promotion of evangelism groups meeting at the church, use ads in *neighborhood* newspapers; public service announcements on radio and television; large signs outside the church; and flyers which can be placed in neighborhood mail boxes by the youth group and distributed after worship services and during rummage sales, bazaars, dinners, and other events.

The large sign posted outside my church the week before each Sunday night evangelism group said, "Hear true stories of a TODAY GOD who acts in lives of people like you—told by the people themselves. THIS SUNDAY NIGHT 6:00 P.M.—supper; 7:00 P.M.—talks." People have come in off the street after reading that!

Use imaginative ways, verbally and visually, to present your invitation. In writing or talking, speak to unchurched and disaffected people on their level. Avoid religious jargon and tell them something about what they can expect. Let them know they are free to take part or just listen, that it is an informal setting, that they may dress casually, that there will not be preaching, that they will not be asked to commit themselves to anything—all conditions that are opposite to the ones in their image of "church"! Be enthusiastic but not intense. Make it understood by your manner that you are not after their membership or money because that is what they think and that turns them off. If you can get them there and offer them something truly meaningful on their level of acceptance, taking them deeper as they progress at their own pace, most searchers eventually will become members and tithers. This is why evangelism groups need to be part of a total parish program.

With clergy and laity sharing responsibility for small groups and all other lay ministry, a church becomes a vital community of Christians and a leaven in society. It becomes a "today church" like the "today God"—one which "acts in lives of people like you."

# 19

# Finding Your Ministries

J UST as every Christian has a unique sacred story, every Christian has at least one ministry for which God has especially gifted him or her.

"God has a ministry for each one of us that is unique and different, for which He has equipped us by temperament, talent and experience," says the Rev. Joseph Dedde, rector of St. Michael and All Angels Episcopal Church, Buffalo. "Our job is to put ourselves at the disposal of the Lord."

There is a spiritual law of giving and receiving which, when allowed to work properly, results in a balanced Christian lifestyle. You can't fulfill your calling to ministry unless you experience spiritual growth, and you can't experience spiritual growth unless you put it into practice through ministry.

You should exercise your ministry not only for your personal contribution to God's work, but for your clergy who need your partnership in fulfilling their ministry, and for your church which needs your participation for it to fulfill its many roles in the lives of its members and in the community. Stressing this point in a sermon at the Episcopal Church of the Advent, Buffalo, the Rev. Robert Eggenschiller said, "This church has two clergy and 400 ministers."

According to one clergyman whose evangelism ministry has

spanned four decades, the most asked question by new Christians is, "Where can I find a church that will feed my soul and help me deal with my problems?" I relate to that because that is what St. Stephen's, Houston, did for me. It fed my soul and in that feeding my problems began to find answers. Church members gave me other kinds of help, such as making connections for me in finding a job and an apartment, but those were secondary to my spiritual needs.

I emphasize this point at every opportunity because there are so many good works being done today by churches in which the clergy and members either are not aware of the unexpressed spiritual needs of those they are helping or they think it is an affront to talk about Jesus Christ to people who go to them for material help. The church is not solely a social agency, although giving material and physical help is part of its ministry. The primary ministries of the church are evangelization of unbelievers and spiritual nurturing of believers.

The Buffalo City Mission is a prime example of a complete Christian ministry. Its clients not only are given meals, clothes and a bed for the night, but they attend a worship service and receive personal counseling with a spiritual emphasis. Those who stay around long enough to seek rehabilitation are put into Bible study groups, given jobs at the mission, and trained in basic skills necessary for job hunting and relating effectively to others.

Some people think of Jesus' teaching to "take up your cross" in terms of sacrificial living. That is part of the meaning but it should not cast an aura of burden around the concept of ministry. I don't claim that ministry is never a burden, but normally it should not be. Ministry should be a joy, imparting a sense of satisfaction and fulfillment—that feeling you get when you know you are in the right place at the right time, using your abilities to help bring to others something they need on the spiritual, emotional, physical or material level. If your ministry is a burden, perhaps you have the wrong attitude toward it, or you are going about it the wrong way, or it is the wrong ministry for you.

The Rev. Bruce Larson, Senior Minister of University Presby-terian Church, Seattle, says, "First, find a ministry you enjoy. I hear people complaining that they have a rotten job to do but somebody must do it for Jesus' sake. I don't buy that approach . . . We need to trust that some of our natural desires and inclinations could also be God's will." This is how it has worked for me. I'm one of those people who has not had to look for ministry. I have always felt a "celestial pull" toward the varied ministries God has given me.

Sometimes others suggest a ministry they think you should do and you need discernment to know if their idea has merit. Such a suggestion may be given because they see some talent in you that should be expressed or because they want to enlist your help in some good work or cause in which they are involved. What is right for them may or may not be right for you. The question is, where does the Lord want *you* to minister!

How can you find your ministries?

First, ask God to show you. Seek His will in prayer. Since this is something He wants you to do, it is logical to assume He will guide you. Usually you will discover one ministry at a time, and often one develops out of another. Also, consult with your clergy and other mature Christians who know you well. Let them work with you in discovering your ministries. Your small group can be an excellent source of guidance and support.

Second, be open to what God shows you. He may guide you into something very unexpected. The idea for one of my "some-times" ministries came to me one day on a trip when I noticed the Gideon Bible in a hotel room. I knew that reading these Bibles had changed people's lives and even prevented suicides. I had heard that pressure had been applied to some hotel chains to remove them. So I took a piece of the hotel stationery and wrote the manager a letter on it after I returned home, expressing thanks for providing the Bible for us. I do this every time I find a Bible in a hotel or motel room. I hope my letter encourages the manager to keep the Bibles in the rooms, and a letter on file is evidence that guests appreciate this service.

God's ways of leading you into ministry may not be what you expected, either. My husband became involved in a ministry at the Niagara County jail for several years because I took him to see a living nativity scene at Niagara United Presbyterian Church, Niagara Falls, N.Y. After viewing the scene, we joined the workers and pastor, the late Rev. Bill Devine, in the kitchen for coffee. We talked for an hour, sharing our Christian experiences and ministries. He told us about his ministry at the jail where he was a chaplain and one of the clergy on the "God Squad" who visited prisoners regularly, counseling and praying with them. He invited my husband to accompany him one night, and so began Ed's jail ministry.

Third, use your spiritual gifts as guidelines. You will discover that you are usually gifted for every ministry God gives you, although you may not discover this until you are involved in it. Ed was very gifted for his jail ministry but he never would have known that if he had not been invited to try it. There are "ministry discovery" questionnaires, such as the one developed by the Anglican Fellowship of Prayer, which can help you discern your spiritual gifts and areas of interest.

One indispensable ingredient in ministry is prayer. Pray to be shown your ministry, pray for guidance in carrying it out, and pray for the ability and wisdom you will need. When you help others, especially on a personal basis, potential pitfalls often will appear, and you can be led into turbulent waters unless you possess the spiritual and emotional maturity to handle the situation. As mentioned in the chapter on Counseling and Prayer (Part I, Chapter 8), some of these pitfalls involve becoming too emotionally involved in another's personal problems, telling another how to solve problems, lending money, and counseling out of your depth.

A difficult situation can arise when some people take advantage of your interest in them by using your time and effort repeatedly to satisfy some emotional or material need, without making any effort to improve their own situation. One such circumstance that happened to me involved a young woman who lived on the other side of town from me in Houston. She would call me late at night, depressed and crying, and ask me to come talk with her. I would get out of bed, dress, drive to her apartment, and listen to her troubles, counseling and praying with her for a couple of hours. Then I would drive home and get up early the next morning to go to work. After I realized that she was doing nothing to help herself, I had to ask the Lord if He wanted me to continue trying to minister to this girl, or if my time and energy would be better used elsewhere. My guidance was to cease the late night visits but welcome her to see me at church.

She drifted away, but the seeds that I and others had planted bore fruit several years later. She wrote to me after I moved to Buffalo; her problems had been resolved. She was happily married to another committed Christian and they were active in church and involved in Christian ministry. One rule for effective ministry is to know when you have given all you have to offer to a person and either refer them to another kind of help or withdraw from the aspect of the relationship that is being misused.

Always pray for people to whom you are ministering, and pray *with* them if appropriate. Prayer undergirds all true ministry, and prayer is a ministry in itself. I often have observed the truth of Archbishop William Temple's statement, "More things are wrought through prayer than man dreams of." There are still orders of nuns who spend most of their time in intercession—a noble ministry and by no means an easy one. Think of the devotion and discipline that requires.

One day in my prayer time, while I was meditating on something I had just read, the thought literally flashed into my mind that "we are co-creators with God in prayer." I was startled by that idea. It was a new idea to me and I had never read it or heard it. I could understand it, though, when I recalled events and healings I either had experienced or witnessed in which there was no explanation but answered prayer. So often Jesus stressed the role of believing prayer in creation of a miracle. Imagine—the Lord of the universe, who could do anything by Himself, allows us to become partners in bringing His will to fruition in our own lives and in the lives of others for whom we pray. Truly, prayer is a powerful ministry!

Since the day I experienced this new insight, I can't count the times I have read it and heard it from others. It has come my way over and over again. Obviously, when God wants His people to understand an idea, He gets the word out!

We all can have an intercession ministry, no matter how busy we are or how physically constrained. Not only can we do this alone but we can share this ministry with a prayer partner on the phone if we can't get together in person. A dear friend, Janet Evans, and I call each other, share what the Lord is doing in our lives, and pray for one another and those for whom we are concerned. In these few minutes each week we share a ministry. She named our little prayer/share group "the conquerors' line."

An important point: there is a difference between ministry and service. Every ministry is a service but not every service is a ministry. Anyone can perform a service without believing in God—and that is good as far as it goes. To a Christian, ministry is more than service because ministry has a spiritual dimension. Make your service a Christian ministry by applying prayer and by witnessing if the opportunity arises. People are hungry for a spiritual understanding of life. They are yearning to experience God's love and to know that they can have a personal relationship with Christ. This is the greatest thing you can share.

# Appendix

Organizations conducting conferences, seminars, missions and renewal weekends and providing printed resources and leadership training in Christian living, prayer, faith sharing, small group development, lay ministry, spiritual healing, church growth, evangelism and education:

*Adventures in Faith* (Episcopal)
Edwin and Joyce Neville
175 Bryant Street
Buffalo, NY 14222     (716) 882-9230
A weekend for renewal in the church by the author of this book and her husband. Includes talks on lay ministry, faith sharing, small groups, prayer, evangelism and Christian discipline; dialogue, discussion groups and ministry discovery exercise. Adaptable for diocesan conferences. Brochure on request.

*Adventures in Ministry (AIM)* (Episcopal)
9753 Quail Hollow Blvd.
Pensacola, FL 32514-5636     (904) 478-5911
Offers a wealth of practical resources for enabling and equipping lay ministers. Keeps a referral list and publishes reports of successful on-going ministries. Creates printed material for use in the congregation. Conducts a comprehensive program for parishes in which participants discover ministry talents, set goals, and consider areas of ministry opportunity. Newsletter, *On Target*. Founder and Executive Director, Dr. Jack M. Ousley.

*Anglican Fellowship of Prayer*
P.O. Box M
Winter Park, FL 32790    (407) 628-4330
  A worldwide organization which conducts conferences, missions, workshops, weekends and retreat days on prayer and prayer group formation. Publications list resources, news, activities, and provide teaching on prayer. Executive Director, Harry Griffith. Coordinator for diocesan representatives, Emily Griffith.

*The Beginning Experience* (Ecumenical)
Central Office—305 Michigan Avenue
Detroit, MI 48226    (313) 965-5110
  A weekend program designed to help the widowed, separated and divorced make a new beginning. Designed to be a time of closure on the past and a new beginning in the present. For persons who are beyond the initial feelings of anger and despair and who are to the point of desiring a new life. Printed material and local contacts provided.

*Bible Reading Fellowship* (Ecumenical)
P.O. Box M
Winter Park, FL 32790    (407) 628-4330
  Comprehensive and systematic programs to meet wide range of Biblical study needs for individuals, families, groups and churches. Commentary, daily devotional reading, current and classic paperbacks, cassettes. Part of worldwide BRF. Executive Director, Harry Griffith.

*Concert of Prayer Project* (Ecumenical)
National Prayer Committee/InterVarsity
6400 Schroeder Road—P.O. Box 7895
Madison, WI 53707-7895    (608) 274-9001
  A two-hour program for church members of all Christian denominations in a city or community who want to pray together for renewal in their area; can be a one-time event or regularly scheduled. Seven basic components. Adaptable to large and small gatherings. Format and instructions provided.

*Creative Evangelism* (Episcopal)
P.O. Box 210643
San Francisco, CA 94121     (415) 321-0887
The Rev. John B. Butcher offers seminars, lectures, weekends and an 8-day Festival of Faith, designed to assist parishes in deepening members' faith and reaching new people through Episcopal style evangelism.

*Chrysalis* (Ecumenical)
P.O. Box 189
Nashville, TN 37202     (615) 340-7227
A three-day event for senior high school students in which they explore how friendship with Jesus can help them live their faith with family, friends, and community. Worship, prayer, fellowship, recreation, singing, discussion. Follow-up groups. Director, Rev. Eugene Blair.

*Cursillo* (Catholic)
National Cursillo Center—P.O. Box 210226
Dallas, TX 75211     (214) 339-6321
An intensive in-depth personal renewal weekend with a group of all men or all women. Five talks a day followed by small group discussions covering subjects from personal piety and grace to ministry in the world. Continuing follow-up growth groups are part of lifelong total program. Executive Director, Gerald P. Hughes.

*Cursillo* (Episcopal)
National Episcopal Cursillo—P.O. Box 213
Cedar Falls, Iowa 50613-0213     (319) 266-5323
The same as the Catholic Cursillo, for Episcopalians.

*Emmaus* (Ecumenical)
P.O. Box 189
Nashville, TN 37202     (615) 340-7227
A three-day weekend for Protestants, modeled after the Catholic Cursillo. For development of Christian leaders who want to strengthen their spiritual lives, deepen understanding of their faith, and live their faith in positions of responsibility in the church and world. Follow-up groups and gatherings. Director, Stephen D. Bryant.

*Emotions Anonymous* (Non-denominational)
P.O. Box 4245
Saint Paul, MN 55104     (612) 647-9712

Similar to AA format, with twelve steps for living a better emotional life; learning to cope with such symptoms as panic, anxiety, depression, abnormal fear, self-pity, resentment, remorse, insomnia, jealousy, envy, guilt, despair, fatigue, tension, boredom, loneliness, low self-esteem, withdrawal, obsessive and negative thinking, worry, compulsive behavior and other psychosomatic illnesses. Also, Youth EA and Children's EA. Catalog of printed resources.

*Engaged Encounter* (Episcopal)
9015 West 11th Street
Wichita, KS 67212     (316) 722-0270

A weekend marriage preparation program for engaged couples. An enjoyable and challenging workshop in practical, daily Christian marriage and family living including decision making, communication skills and marital spirituality.

*Episcopal Center for Evangelism*
P.O. Box 920
Live Oak, FL 32060     (904) 963-2199

Missions and workshops on personal and parish renewal, evangelism, church growth, gifts and fruits of the Spirit, and allied subjects, offered by the Very Rev. Robert B. Hall, the Center's Founder, and his wife, Marjorie. Newsletter, *Refreshment,* runs articles on spiritual growth, church growth and resources.

*Episcopal Committee on Religion and Freedom*
8609 Cottage Street
Vienna, VA 22180     (703) 573-7256

Education for lay ministry in the decision making bodies of church and state, based on the premise that religion is best expressed in a free society. Chairman, Frank Watson. Affiliated with the Institute on Religion and Democracy, Washington, D.C.

*Exodus International—North America* (Ecumenical)
P.O. Box 2121
San Rafael, CA 94912    (415) 454-1017
    A switchboard, resource and support network for a multiplicity of organizations, churches and individuals with a Christian ministry to men and women who want to come out of the homosexual lifestyle. Referral service and educational printed materials.

*Faith Alive Weekend* (Episcopal, services other churches by request)
P.O. Box 1987
York, PA 17405    (717) 848-2137
    An event for the whole church family, married and single, of all ages. Concurrent program for adults, youth, and children from age 6, each with its own coordinator. Led by a team of lay persons, it takes place at the parish church. Emphasis on personal relationship with Christ, commitment, prayer, renewal. Faith sharing, prayer, discussion; no teaching or Bible study. Follow-up weekend, Venture in Faith, centers on Bible study. Executive Director, Thomas G. Riley.

*Faith/At/Work* (Ecumenical)
11065 Little Patuxent Parkway
Columbia, MD 21044    (301) 730-3690
    Holds conferences, women's events and leadership training workshops, led by clergy and laity, in cities and centers around the U.S. and Canada. Wide variety of formats and subjects including small group development, ministry discovery, healing of emotions, women in ordained ministry, Christian relating in family and profession, spiritual growth, and more. Combines scripturally based teaching and participant interaction. Bi-monthly magazine, *Faith/At/Work,* provides resources, book reviews, events listings, articles on innovative ministries and church programs, and stories of personal witness.

*Fine Arts Contemporary Evangelism (FACE)* (Episcopal)
2716 Market Avenue, North
Canton, Ohio 44714    (216) 455-1689
    Artist Gordon Kelly presents a visual and verbal encounter with the life and teachings of Christ, relating Biblical content and imagery to

contemporary situations. Provides programs for teaching missions, retreats, Sunday worship, church school classes, church suppers, Lenten and Advent series.

*The Fisherfolk* (Episcopal)
P.O. Box 309
Aliquippa, PA 15001-9900      1-800-722-4879
   Young adult music teams which travel to local parishes, diocesan events, and regional gatherings, offering concerts, worship conferences, and music leadership at Sunday Eucharists. Blend contemporary and traditional music in a gentle, joyful style. Fisherfolk home base is The Community of Celebration where their Training Institute offers conferences for church leaders on worship and parish life.

*FOCUS—Fellowship of Christians in Universities and Schools*
139 East Putnam Avenue
Greenwich, CT 06830      (203) 622-0430
   An ecumenical ministry to students in nearly 100 independent schools in 14 states. FOCUS provides both on-campus and off-campus speakers, small groups, Bible studies, retreats, and more than 15 conferences for prep students and faculty each year at ski weeks, colleges, and the FOCUS Study Center on Martha's Vineyard, MA. Director, Roger Dewey.

*Happening* (Episcopal)
P.O. Box 225
Suamico, WI 54173      (414) 434-2247
   A weekend for high school youth through which spirituality may be developed, lived and shared. Discussion of Christ's teachings in a joyful setting which includes singing sessions and informal gatherings. Provides a means to continue the Christian formation begun at the weekend, encouraging participants to make a friend, be a friend, and bring a friend to Christ. Executive Director, the Rev. Wayne Bulloch.

*Heartbeat Evangelistic Ministries* (Episcopal—Ecumenical)
P.O. Box 101026
Pittsburgh, PA 15237      (412) 322-4040
   The Rev. John Dowker, Anglican evangelist, offers single preaching

engagements, training sessions for lay witnessing, evangelistic workshops for clergy, evangelistic missions in the local church, and evangelistic crusades.

*Institute for American Church Growth* (Ecumenical)
2670 S. Myrtle Avenue, Suite 201
Monrovia, CA 91016     (818) 447-2112
   Helps churches develop new strategies for outreach and growth geared toward church growth, Christian education, lay ministry and evangelism as the ways to build a viable Christian community which will continually attract new people. Based on information researched from successful churches of various denominations. Founder and President, Dr. Win Arn.

*International Order of St. Luke the Physician* (Ecumenical)
P.O. Box 13701
San Antonio, TX 78213     (512) 342-4261
   OSL's purpose is to promote the healing ministry in the churches. It sponsors local chapters whose clerical and lay members meet regularly for intercession and study of prayer and healing. Conducts healing missions, provides speakers and resources. Publishes *Sharing* magazine.

*John Guest Evangelistic Team* (Ecumenical)
3366 Burton, S.E.
Grand Rapids, MI 49506     (616) 942-5600
   "Renewing your church as you reach your community" is the purpose of the John Guest city-wide crusade involving typically 75-100 churches of many denominations. The Rev. Guest, an Episcopal priest with two doctoral degrees, is widely known for his powerful speaking style and has been called "the thinking man's evangelist." The Team helps local churches organize.

*King-Bay Chaplaincy* (Ecumenical)
Box 175, Toronto Dominion Centre
Toronto, Ontario M5K 1H6     (416) 366-0818
   An inter-church ministry to the business and professional community in downtown Toronto. Equips church people to apply Christian values in daily decision making through groups for Bible study, discussion and

prayer. Shares Christian faith in the workplace through public forums, worship and outreach programs. Seminars on stress, career crises, personal relationships, values and ethics. Personal counseling, referral service, lay ministry development. Discovery Weekend for deeper experience. Development and implementation of value-based management programs for companies. Newsletter, *The Communicator*. Chaplain, the Rev. Graham H. Tucker.

*Lay Renewal Ministries* (Ecumenical)
P.O. Box 16807
St. Louis, MO 63105     (314) 727-0033, 1-800-241-8581
    A resource for motivating and equipping lay men and women for ministry in their local churches, and for helping pastors and church leaders plan for total renewal. Conducts five-day Lay Renewal event; weekend events—Lay Witness Mission, Abundant Life Mission, Marriage Renewal, and an Officer Retreat motivational workshop for officers, key and potential church leaders, and spouses. Provides consultants, speakers, printed and video resources for self-conducted programs for Advent, Lent, Stewardship, Discipleship, Bible study, youth and children's programs, etc. Affiliated with National Association of Evangelicals. Director, Bob Fenn.

*Lay Witness Mission* (United Methodist)
United Methodist General Board of Discipleship
P.O. Box 840
Nashville, TN 37202     (615) 340-7120
    A faith sharing weekend for United Methodist and other churches; similar to Faith Alive Weekend. Follow-ups: Venture in Discipleship Weekend; Discipleship Celebration Weekend; Visitation: Caring Evangelism (a 6-session training); Faith-Sharing (a 4-session training). Director, Shirley F. Clement.

*Marriage Encounter* (Catholic)
*Worldwide Marriage Encounter*          *National Marriage Encounter*
1908 E. Highland Avenue, Suite A     4704 Jamerson Place
San Bernardino, CA 92404             Orlando, FL 32807
    Or contact the Family Life Department of the local diocese.
    A weekend at a retreat center for married couples who want to enrich

and deepen their relationship. Includes teaching of effective communication, personal conversations between husband and wife, and small group discussions. Designed to inspire couples to look at themselves as persons, at their marriage relationship, their relationship to God and to the world around them. *Worldwide* has an intensive emphasis on Catholic faith and relationships; very structured. *National* has an ecumenical emphasis—Protestants welcomed; less structured, more informal.

*Marriage Encounter* (Episcopal)
9015 West 11th Street
Wichita, KS 67212     (316) 722-0270
   The same as the Catholic Marriage Encounter, for Episcopalians. For clergy and laity. Members of other Christian denominations and the unchurched welcomed.

*People Plus* (Episcopal)
7216 Valley Drive
Bettendorf, Iowa 52722     (319) 332-4820
   Provides manual for leader to follow in conducting 3½ day summer sessions for small groups of pre-adolescents. Experiences of an educational and spiritually renewing nature, integrating gospel message with activities that build self-esteem. Discussions center on self-identity, friends, family, peer influence, change, God's forgiveness, prayer. Consultant available. Program Directors, Jim and Miriam Ingram.

*The Pittsburgh Experiment* (Ecumenical)
*The Guideposts National Experiment* (Ecumenical)
1802 Investment Building
Pittsburgh, PA 15222     (412) 281-9578
   Ministry to business and industrial sectors through small prayer/share/support groups in the marketplace; since 1955. Weekly meetings during lunch, before and after work, of up to twelve people who share what is happening in their lives—answered prayer, new insights, problems, successes and failures—and who pray together. Employment Anonymous groups were formed in 1962 to minister to the unemployed in the same format. Executive Director, the Rev. Paul F. Everett.

Affiliated with The Guideposts National Experiment as the result of requests for Experiment groups in other cities.

*School of Pastoral Care* (Ecumenical)

| | |
|---|---|
| The Rev. Charles Boole | The Rev. Edward A. Rouffy |
| International President | Vice President |
| 140 Hall Avenue East | P.O. Box 96 |
| Renfrew, Ontario K7V 2S4 | Castle Rock, CO 80104 |
| (613) 432-3062, 432-2127 | (303) 688-5185 |

Conducts intensive five-day teaching conferences for professionals and laity in religious and health care fields. Purpose is to provide a deeper understanding of the use of spiritual therapy in the healing of physical, mental, spiritual and social ills. Healing of the whole person is stressed. Opportunity for personal counseling and prayer.

*Vocare* (Episcopal)
Route, 1, Box 207
Brownsville, WI 53006     (414) 583-3003

A renewal weekend for young adults ages 18-26, when they are in the decade after high school, facing many serious decisions which set the direction for much of their adult life. "Vocare" comes from the Latin word meaning "to call." *Vocare* centers on the question of vocation—"What is God calling me to do with my life?" Patterned after Cursillo and staffed by college age people and clergy. Director, Peter R. Bird.

*Windsong Ministries* (Episcopal)
Route 2, Box 2511
Townsend, Georgia 31331     (912) 832-4602

The Very Rev. David B. and Ginny Collins lead healing missions, renewal conferences, retreats, prayer workshops, teaching and preaching missions. Newsletter, *Windsong Ministries.*

*Youth Encounter Spirit (YES)* (Ecumenical)
The Conant Family
77 MacFarland Avenue
Ivyland, PA 18974     (215) 322-5938

Provides a weekend experience, Youth Encounter, for "all persons between the ages of 12 and 16," and a one-day experience, Mini-Encounter, for children ages 7-11. Three major themes are: encounter with self, others, and God. Conducted by a team of trained YE leaders, Marriage Encounter couples and clergy.

*Christian Healing Ministries, Inc.*
438 West 67th Street—P.O. Box 9520
Jacksonville, FL 32208     (904) 765-3332

Francis MacNutt, Ph.D., founder of the Association of Christian Therapists, and his wife, Judith Sewell MacNutt, a psychotherapist and founder of Christian Counseling Services, share a ministry of deep inner healing in a range of severe problems. At their Christian Healing Center and in conferences around the country, they and other members of their team combine teaching, prayer and counseling therapy for healing of emotional, mental and physical conditions. Specialized areas include painful memories, emotional dependence, dysfunctional families, eating disorders, alcoholism, drug abuse and compulsive sexuality. A main component of the MacNutts' ministry is the teaching and practice of the principles of physical healing through prayer. Books by the MacNutts and others in these fields are available from their bookstore.

# Notes

**Part I/Chapter I**

1 Claxton Monro and William S. Taegel, *Witnessing Laymen Make Living Churches* (Waco, Tex.: Word Books, 1968), p. 21.

2 The Rev. A. Wayne Schwab, *Some Basic Learnings About Evangelism and Renewal* (New York City: The Executive Council of the Episcopal Church, Epiphany, 1977).

3 Rosalind Rinker, *You Can Witness With Confidence* (Grand Rapids, Mich.: Zondervan, 1966), p. 43.

4 *Creating Christian Cells,* rev. ed. (Faith/At/Work, Inc.; 11065 Little Patuxent Parkway, Columbia, Md. 21044; 1951).

5 The Rev. Douglas C. Blackwell, editor, *Relay,* periodical of the Aurora Conference Centre, Aurora, Ontario, vol. 3, no. 1.

**Part I/Chapter 2**

1 Rosalind Rinker and Harry C. Griffith, *Sharing God's Love* (Grand Rapids, Mich.: Zondervan, 1976), p. 8.

**Part I/Chapter 3**

1 *Webster's New Collegiate Dictionary* (Springfield, Mass.: G. & C. Merriam Co., 1949), p. 984.

**Part I/Chapter 5**

1 Rinker, *You Can Witness With Confidence,* p. 36.

2 "Dear Father Hanner," *New Life* (December 1975), pp. 5-7.

**Part I/Chapter 6**

1 Robert Benjamin Hall, *Sharing Your Faith: A Course in Lay Witnessing* (York, Pa.: The Brotherhood of St. Andrew, 1973), p. 51.

2 Ibid., p. 52.

3 Ibid., p. 47.

4 Ibid., p. 42.

5 Ibid., p. 45.

6 Ibid., p. 43.

**Part I/Chapter 7**
1 Rinker, *You Can Witness With Confidence,* p. 49.
2 Ibid., p. 36.
3 Hall, *Sharing Your Faith,* p. 49.

**Part I/Chapter 8**
1 Edwin L. Neville, Jr., Ph.D., from a talk given at a seminar on lay ministry at St. Peter's Episcopal Church, Niagara Falls, N.Y., 6 November 1976, and published under the title, "Then and There Prayers," *Faith/At/Work,* February 1978, p. 5.

**Part I/Chapter 9**
1 Rinker and Griffith, *Sharing God's Love,* p. 60.

**Part I/Chapter 10**
1 *Faith/At/Work,* September 1961.
2 Monro and Taegel, *Witnessing Laymen Make Living Churches,* p. 169.
3 Ibid., pp. 183-84.
4 Alan Richardson, ed., *A Theological Wordbook of the Bible* (New York: Macmillan, 1964), pp. 179-81.
5 Monro and Taegel, *Witnessing Laymen Make Living Churches,* p. 14.
6 *Faith/At/Work,* September 1961.

**Part II/Chapter 1**
1 *Creating Christian Cells,* p. 6.
2 Ibid., p. 7.

**Part II/Chapter 2**
1 Helen Smith Shoemaker, *Schools of Prayer for Leaders and Learners* (published by Helen Smith Shoemaker; Burnside, Md. 21153; n.d.) p. 37.
2 Ibid.

74235